This Book Belongs To

Christmas
Book 2

Content and Artwork by **Gooseberry Patch Company**

LEISURE ARTS
Vice President and Editor-in-Chief: Anne Van Wagner Childs
Executive Director: Sandra Graham Case
Administrative Coordinator: Debra Nettles
Special Projects Designer: Patricia Wallenfang Sowers
Design Director: Cyndi Hansen
Test Kitchen Director/Foods Editor: Celia Fahr Harkey, R.D.
Editorial Director: Susan Frantz Wiles
Publications Director: Kristine Anderson Mertes
Creative Art Director: Gloria Bearden
Licensed Product Coordinator: Lisa Truxton Curton

EDITORIAL STAFF

EDITORIAL
Managing Editor: Linda L. Trimble
Associate Editors: Darla Burdette Kelsay and
    Suzie Puckett

TECHNICAL
Senior Technical Writer: Theresa Hicks Young
Technical Writers: Jennifer S. Hutchings, Barbara
    Marguerite McClintock, K.J. Smith and Marley N. Washum
Copy Editor: Susan Frazier
Production Assistant: Sharon Gillam

FOODS
Assistant Foods Editor: Jane Kenner Prather
Foods Copy Editor: Judy Millard
Test Kitchen Home Economists: Pat Coker and
    Rose Glass Klein
Test Kitchen Coordinator: Nora Faye Taylor

DESIGN
Designers: Polly Tullis Browning, Diana Sanders Cates,
    Cherece Athy Cooper, Sandra Spotts Ritchie, Billie Steward,
    Anne Pulliam Stocks and Linda Diehl Tiano
Executive Assistant: Debra Smith

ART
Book/Magazine Graphic Art Director: Diane M. Thomas
Senior Graphic Artist: Linda Lovette Smart
Graphic Artists: Faith R. Lloyd, Diana Sanders and Robin Walters
Color Technician: Mark Hawkins
Staff Photographer: Russell Ganser
Photography Stylists: Karen Smart Hall, Tiffany Huffman,
    Elizabeth Lackey, and Janna Laughlin
Publishing Systems Administrator: Becky Riddle
Publishing Systems Assistants: Myra S. Means and
    Chris Wertenberger

PROMOTIONS
Managing Editor: Alan Caudle
Associate Editor: Steven M. Cooper
Designer and Graphic Artist: Dale Rowett
Art Operations Director: Jeff Curtis
Graphic Artist: Deborah Kelly

BUSINESS STAFF
Publisher: Rick Barton
Vice President, Finance: Tom Siebenmorgen
Vice President, Retail Marketing: Bob Humphrey
Director of Corporate Planning and Development:
    Laticia Mull Cornett
Vice President, National Accounts: Pam Stebbins
Retail Marketing Director: Margaret Sweetin
General Merchandise Manager: Cathy Laird
Vice President, Operations: Jim Dittrich
Distribution Director: Rob Thieme
Retail Customer Service Manager: Wanda Price
Print Production Manager: Fred F. Pruss

Library of Congress Catalog Number 99-71586
Hardcover ISBN 1-57486-197-2
Softcover ISBN 1-57486-198-0

10 9 8 7 6 5 4 3

Christmas

Book 2

A LEISURE ARTS PUBLICATION

Christmas

Gooseberry Patch

From our family to yours, a collection of best-loved recipes, gifts from the heart and holiday decorating ideas.

How Did Gooseberry Patch Get Started?

You may know the story of Gooseberry Patch...the tale of two country friends who decided one day over the backyard fence to try their hands at the mail order business. Started in JoAnn's kitchen back in 1984, Vickie & JoAnn's dream of a "Country Store in Your Mailbox" has grown and grown to a 96-page catalog with over 400 products, including cookie cutters, Santas, snowmen, gift baskets, angels and our very own line of cookbooks! What an adventure for two country friends!

Through our catalogs and books, Gooseberry Patch has met country friends from all over the world. While sharing letters and phone calls, we found that our friends love to cook, decorate, garden and craft. We've created Kate, Holly & Mary Elizabeth to represent these devoted friends who live and love the country lifestyle the way we do. They're just like you & me... they're our "Country Friends®!"

Your friends at Gooseberry Patch

Holly Mary Elizabeth Kate Spotty

Just For You

Contents

Catch the Christmas Spirit!

Credits

We want to extend a warm *thank you* to the people who allowed us to photograph our projects at their homes: John and Anne Childs, Tim and Janna Laughlin, Charles and Peg Mills and Duncan and Nancy Porter.

We want to especially thank photographers Mark Mathews, Larry Pennington, Andy Uilkie and Ken West of Peerless Photography and Jerry R. Davis of Jerry Davis Photography, all of Little Rock, Arkansas, for their excellent work.

To Wisconsin Technicolor LLC, of Pewaukee, Wisconsin, we say *thank you* for the superb color reproduction and excellent pre-press preparation.

To Lynn Busa, who created the cross stitch designs for the following projects in this book, we extend a special word of thanks: *Santa Pillow*, 28; *Reindeer Pillow*, 29; *Snowman Pillow*, 29; *Cross-Stitched Snowman Ornament*, 30; *Santa Wall Hanging*, 30; and *Reindeer Feed Bag*, 31.

Thanks also go to Amy Bassett, Ruth Ann Epperson, Phyllis Lundy, Gail Sharp and Lavonne Sims, who assisted in making and testing some of the projects in this book.

All's well that ends well. *old adage*

Heart Felt and Hand made

GIFTS that TASTE GOOD

Savor the Flavor of Christmas

Catch the Christmas Spirit!

It's never too early to catch the Christmas spirit! Get ready for the most festive time of the year...pass around pictures of holidays past, enjoy your Yuletide collectibles, deck the halls (and the tree!), address your Christmas cards and have each family member start their "wish list." Above all, enjoy the magic of the season!

Painted paper maché boxes are perfect for storing photographs! You can add special touches to personalize.
Turn to page 120 for instructions.

Vickie's Photo Boxes

When family and friends drop by during the holidays, take an instant snapshot of them by the tree. Decorate the edges of the photo with glued-on trims...greenery, colorful paper borders, festive stickers...and use a marker to add the visitors' names and the date at the bottom. Voilà! A personalized, dated ornament!

Keep all your Christmas photos in special albums. At Thanksgiving each year, bring out all those memories from years past...a great start to the holidays! Leave them out all season long for family and friends to enjoy.

Antiqued black & white photocopies of treasured snapshots create a nostalgic feel on the family photos box. Instructions are on page 120.

Pets are family too! Dress up precut mats to frame favorite photos; tuck among the tree branches. Instructions are on page 120.

an Idea or two:

● COVER A RECIPE-SIZE BOX WITH GRANNY'S FAMILY RECIPES & GRANNY'S PHOTO!

● PUT A KEEPSAKE TEA CUP OR OTHER RELIC TO PASS DOWN IN A BOX COVERED WITH FAMILY PHOTOGRAPHS—GIVE IT TO SOMEONE DEAR IN THE NEXT GENERATION.

Include your pets in your celebrations. Hang a wreath and twinkling lights on the doghouse, put a little jingle bell on Kitty's collar or tie a Christmas bandanna around Fido's neck.

Poinsettias are lovely, but they're also poisonous to our animal friends. If you have indoor pets, purchase silk poinsettias instead.

Wear something festive! Jingle bells on shoe laces, Christmas balls for earrings, glittery sweaters, colorful socks or a Santa hat…all will lift your spirit as well as those of folks around you!

Have some fun going through family photo albums ∽ and more fun putting those old pictures to good use!

★

Pull out favorite old pix and have them photocopied on a color copier. You can make them different sizes; reduce to 50% or 75%. Put as many photos on each copy as you can — you're going to cut them apart. Go ahead and get a few copies ∽ you will use a LOT with this good idea.

★

Vickie likes using copies of nostalgic old black & white photos ∽ they look terrific on kraft-colored paper maché boxes.

Remember your animal friends at Christmas...

★ Hang up Stockings filled with treats.

★ Decorate the Litter Box.

★ Get Spotty a red collar & leash.

Animals are such agreeable friends — they ask no questions, they pass no criticisms.
— George Eliot

GOOD & LOYAL ★ FRIENDS ★ GOOD & LOYAL

★ For the Birds: Melt suet over low heat & stir in mixed bird seed. Pour into foil-lined jelly roll pan. Chill. Cut out shapes with cookie cutters. Insert wire hook for hanging in trees.

★ Make a special holiday placemat for under pet dishes.

★ Donate to your local humane society.

Stitch up simple felt stockings to hold treats and toys for your pets. Instructions are on page 120.

Do you have a collection of Teddy bears? Dress them up in festive style! Instructions for the Santa and angel costumes are on page 121.

Create a "beary" fun welcoming committee! Gather your favorite teddies and arrange them on a table in your entryway. Add greenery, festively wrapped packages, etc.

A fire in the fireplace says "welcome." Keep several dry logs nearby as well as a bucketful of cinnamon pine cones for a quick country fire. The heat from the fire will scent the entire room with cinnamon.

Do you have a child returning home for the holidays? Give a rousing welcome by decorating his or her bedroom with twinkly colored lights!

"The holly's up, the house is bright, the tree is ready, the candles alight."

— Old German Carol

Instead of piling this year's cards on a table, show them off on a rustic garland! Instructions for the primitive Santa clips are on page 121.

Don't throw away those beautiful cards...use them to create your own ornaments and package tie-ons. Cut off the back of the card and trim around the picture if you wish. Punch a small hole at the top. Lightly coat with spray adhesive and dust with glitter for all-over sparkle, or use a glue stick to highlight certain areas. Sprinkle on the glitter, then shake the excess onto a newspaper. Thread a piece of raffia, twine or ribbon through the hole and you have a wonderful ornament or darling package tie-on!

On a dreary day, set up an "art table" for the kids...stock it with rubber stamps, brown paper grocery bags and envelopes. They'll have a ball stamping Christmas cards and making customized gift wrap, and you can take care of some of the items on your to-do list!

Spotty strings jute across his windows & mantel and hangs up his Christmas cards with painted clip clothespins.

Display a collage of pretty cards beneath the glass on a glass-topped table!

Mary Elizabeth volunteers to head up an afternoon of holiday crafts at her local school. (she's a brave soul)

Gather the family by the fire and have everyone share a favorite memory of past holidays. Make a videotape to share with far-away loved ones.

Have a clothing and old toy round-up with your family. Giving away "gently worn" and outgrown clothes and toys is a wonderful way to share the Christmas spirit.

On the day after Thanksgiving, get everyone together to trim the tree! Play Christmas carols, sip cocoa and catch the merry spirit!

All hearts come home for Christmas…and for a lasting memory, make a sentimental autographed pillow sham. Have friends and family members sign a ready-made sham; then embroider over their signatures. Be sure to date the back! *Turn to page 121 for instructions.*

It's Beginning to Look A Lot Like Christmas!

Kate, Holly & Mary Elizabeth just can't wait to decorate for the holidays, and they've got lots of new ideas to share! Mary Elizabeth likes to start in the kitchen with a tiny tree and decorated jars to hold home-baked goodies. Holly's first order of business is to make a new wreath for the front door, and Kate plans to make a flurry of snowmen to scatter all over the house. You'll want to start early to deck your halls in style!

For a natural greeting, cover a wreath with pine, cedar and boxwood; finish with dried apples, pomegranates and cinnamon sticks. Instructions begin on page 122.

Welcoming wreaths

Nothing says "Welcome" like a wreath on the door…or in the window or on the wall! Use a little imagination and crafting know-how to make your own one-of-a kind wreaths.

Take a stroll through your own backyard to gather items for this woodsy wreath! Add a big bow and a pair of deer to finish; see instructions on page 122.

Clusters of bright red berries make a colorful splash on a fresh pine wreath. Instructions begin on page 122.

Make a Fresh Pine Wreath

You'll need:

★ 12" double-rail wire wreath form
★ 22 gauge reel wire on spool
★ 3 to 5 pine cones
★ Pruning shears & wire cutters
★ assortment of fresh greens, cut into 6" lengths ~ I like to use pine, boxwood, holly or shrubbery trimmings
★ bow w/9" tails

First, Make a hanger on wreath form using a double-thickness of wire. Attach one end of wire to form, leaving a tail to tie off when finished.

Next, lay 3 or 4 pieces of greens on the form in a fan-shape. Wrap wire around stem ends a couple of times to secure them to form.

Covering the previous stems & wire, lay 3 or 4 more pieces of greenery in a fan-shape on the wreath form. Secure with reel wire. Keep going until entire form is covered with greens. For variety & visual interest, you can vary the greens you're using by color & texture.

Just say Snow!

If you just can't wait for the first snow of the season, let these jolly snow folk add wintry fun to your home. You can give guests a heart-melting greeting and trim a tree for your entryway…or choose some of our other frosty decorations. Instructions for the Snow-Couple Door Basket below and other projects begin on page 122.

Love, and do what you Like.
— Saint Augustine

Make snow days extra special for the kids…tell stories, go sledding, make cocoa, sing Christmas carols, watch Christmas movies and wrap presents.

We decorated this cute tabletop tree with the Snow-Couple Bells from page 25 and the twig snowflowers from the Snowflake Garden on page 24.

Kate's Snow-man Topiaries

...Tabletop guys to greet winter guests!

These little snow folk are each as unique as the members of a family! For the simple instructions, turn to page 122.

turn to page 122.

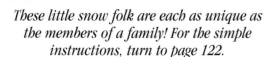

Make a

whole family!

SNOWFLAKE GARDEN

Winter's abloom in an old wooden planter box! Paint the box red, then spray it with wood-tone spray for a "gently-aged" look. Use dimensional paint to draw a snowflake or two and write "Snowflake Garden" on the box. For each snowflower, hot glue three crisscrossed twigs together. Wrap the center with wire, then wire to a stick stem; spray paint it white. Fill the bottom of the box with floral foam, then add lots of fresh pine greenery for that Christmasy-smell. Arrange the snowflowers, some "snow-tipped" pine cones and a few red berries in the garden.

Remember when you were a little kid and right after a snowfall, what fun you had? Couldn't you still just lick your lips for a snow cone made with freshly fallen snow? Or, how about making snow angels or building a snowman? Remember how good it felt to come inside, fingers and toes stinging from the cold, to take off those frosty boots, sit by the fire and sip a cup of hot cocoa? Find that little kid inside you and relive some of your happiest childhood memories!
Vickie

Have your kids ever asked you how Santa knows if they're naughty or nice? The answer is easy. The birds know. All year long the birds keep a watch over all the children of the world. We all know that the animals can talk to Santa, so the birds fly to the North Pole and report their findings. Birds can be sitting high in a tree and watching you play in the yard, or they can peek in your window to see if you went to bed on time or did the chores you were told.
Wendy Lee Paffenroth
Pine Island, NY

Snow Couple

YOU WILL NEED:
- ★ 2 · 6½" SQUARE PIECES COTTON BATTING
- ★ 1 · 4" x 4" PIECE OF BLACK FELT
- ★ 2 · TINY JINGLE BELLS
- ★ 2 · 1¾" DIAMETER CLAY POTS
- ★ 2 · 6" x 1" HOMESPUN SCRAPS
- ★ 2 · 14" LONG PIECES LIGHT·WEIGHT WIRE
- ★ 4 · 1" CINNAMON STICKS
- ★ 4 · BUTTONS
- ★ 2 · 1" DIAMETER WOODEN BALLS
- ★ WHITE, BLACK & ORANGE PAINT
- ★ SMALL BRUSH
- ★ SCISSORS
- ★ HEAVY THREAD
- ★ SEWING NEEDLE and
- ★ GLUE

Here are your 5 pattern pieces:

- ★ Hat Crown
- ★ Hat Top
- ★ Hat Brim
- ★ Body Circle
- ★ Ear Muffs

Cool!

Here's something to smile about…this fun couple is super easy to craft using tiny clay pots wrapped with cotton batting. *Instructions continued on page 123.*

Cheery painted chairs

Set your imagination free to create these cheerful chairs! Paint them in bright colors and cover the seats with festive fabrics. Even Santa will be impressed!

CHEERY CHAIR ORNAMENT

- 7½-inch tall wooden chair
- spray primer
- white, yellow, red and green acrylic paint
- paintbrushes
- small star stencils
- wood-tone spray
- clear acrylic spray sealer
- fabric for seat cover
- hot glue gun

Refer to Painting Techniques, page 131, for some painting tips from your Country Friends®. Allow primer, paint, wood-tone spray and sealer to dry after each application.

1. Spray chair with primer. Paint wooden parts of the chair desired Base Color.

(continued on page 123)

With a little paint and fabric, you'll create a chair so festive that even Santa will be tempted to sit back and take a break from his Christmas Eve deliveries. Instructions are on page 123.

Santa

Let Santa and some of his favorite friends bring country charm to your decor!

CROSS-STITCHED PILLOWS
- embroidery floss (see color key for desired design, pages 137-139)
- 6¼-inch square of Fiddler's Cloth (14-ct)
- red and green fabrics
- stencil plastic
- quilt marking pencil
- ¼-inch dia. cotton cord
- polyester fiberfill

Refer to Cross Stitch, page 130, before beginning project. For all sewing, match right sides and raw edges and use a ¼-inch seam allowance, unless otherwise indicated. Wash, dry and press all red and green fabrics to be used for pillows.

1. For each pillow, using 2 strands of floss for *Cross Stitches* and one strand of floss for *Backstitches* and *French Knots*, center and stitch desired design, pages 137-139, on cloth.

2. Follow **Pillow Top** instructions to add fabric borders to stitched piece.

Santa or Reindeer Pillow Top
1. Cut 6 red and 6 green 11/2"x15" strips from fabrics.

(continued on page 124)

and Friends

CROSS-STITCHED SNOWMAN ORNAMENT

- embroidery floss (see color key, page 137)
- perforated plastic canvas (14-ct)
- red raffia
- hot glue gun

Refer to Cross Stitch, page 130, before beginning project.

1. Omitting the heart border and using 2 strands of floss for *Cross Stitches* and one strand of floss for *Backstitches* and *French Knots*, center and stitch snowman design, page 137, on perforated plastic.

2. Cut out ornament one thread outside stitched design. For hanger, fold raffia in half and glue ends to back of ornament.

With cheery Christmas songs playing in the background, you'll have a ball stitching a wall hanging, a tree ornament and a reindeer "feed bag." Instructions for the wall hanging are on page 124.

*S*how off your handiwork! Fill a miniature tree with cross-stitched ornaments. Stitch merry motifs on tiny bags and fill with goodies…candy canes, little gifts or greenery.

REINDEER FEED BAG

- embroidery floss (see color key, page 138)
- 24"x27" piece of Klostern
- small twigs from the yard
- miniature artificial apple picks
- preserved juniper
- floral tape
- one inch wide ribbon

Refer to Cross Stitch, page 130, before beginning project. Separate strands of floss and realign before stitching. Use a ½-inch seam allowance for all sewing unless otherwise indicated.

1. Using 9 strands of floss for *Cross Stitches*, 3 strands of floss for *Backstitches* and 4 strands of floss for *French Knots*, work reindeer design, page 138, on Klostern with bottom of design 4½ inches from bottom of fabric and centered between short edges.

(continued on page 125)

Holiday MAGIC

Create a magical mood for your holiday table with an appliquéd table runner, place cards and napkins. A tiny tree trimmed with stockings and stars makes a great country centerpiece. Instructions begin on page 125.

33

Plenty o' POTS

Don't hide those old flowerpots in the gardening shed! Decorate them in holiday style and use them to hold greenery, pine cones and even gifts. Put on your painting clothes, grab a paintbrush and have a holly-jolly good time!

FESTIVE POTS

Spray the flowerpots with a coat of primer, then paint the rim, base and inside with desired colors of acrylic paint. Let the first coat dry thoroughly before adding a second coat. Referring to *Painting Techniques*, page 131,

PLENTY O' POTS * POTS * PLENTY O' POTS *

for some painting tips from your Country Friends® and using the patterns, page 141, to cut desired shapes from compressed craft sponges, decorate the pots with *Sponge Painted* shapes and highlights and hand-painted details. Use a permanent marker to write messages or draw some "stitched" outlines...seal the pots with water-based sealer. After the pots are dry, glue on buttons, bows, raffia or greenery for that touch of country charm.

35

A Homespun CHRISTMAS

Bring a truly old-fashioned feel to Christmas by decorating with lots of simple items you can easily find or make…pine cones, citrus peel cut-outs, dried apple and orange slices, fresh cranberries, greenery and homespun bows.

PINE CONE CANDLEHOLDERS

Take the kids pine cone hunting. Snip the tops from assorted-size pine cones…make sure they will sit flat. Cut your candles to desired heights and glue them in the pine cones. Arrange the candleholders in a tart tin filled with dried apple slices, rose hips, cranberries and star anise. Enjoy the warm glow…but remember Grandma's friendly advice, "Never leave burning candles unattended."

"Tis the season for cold winter noses, cheeks red as roses and warm, happy hearts."
— Tessa Adelman

This tabletop tree is a natural…decorated with dried citrus peel cut-outs, apple slices, pine cones, pomegranates and other simple ornaments from nature! See page 126 for instructions.

BOX OF NATURALS

Citrusy scents fill the air from this fragrant arrangement of wintry goodies. Simply arrange cinnamon sticks, dried tangerines, quince and apple slices, star anise, cranberries, pomegranates and some fresh pine in a wooden box. Tie with a gingham bow and you've made a delightful holiday centerpiece!

GARLAND OF GOODIES

Make your own terrific fragrant garlands. Glue your favorite Garland Goodies to a length of raffia…you can even add some citrus peel cut-outs for a scent of orange.

GARLAND ★ GOODIES:

cinnamon sticks
miniature indian corn
whole nuts
tiny baskets
bay leaves
pine cones
homespun fabric
star anise
gingerbread shapes
fresh herbs
dried fruit slices

(You might need to make holes with a drill in some items before stringing.)

Greet guests with this beautiful handmade wreath; it's easy. Start with a twig wreath and glue on layers of lemon leaves, pine cones, dried fruits and other trims from the Garland Goodies list above; finish with a plump plaid bow!

Here's A Neat idea!

Dried Citrus peel cut-outs

Cut moist peel with 1" to 1½" cookie cutters. (Stars & Hearts look wonderful in a garland or bowl of potpourri!) To form holes for garland string, insert a toothpick in peel cut-out where hole is needed, and remove pick when cut-out is completely dry. Air-drying works best, and cut-outs should be dry in 7 to 10 days. If peel starts to curl up, you might want to add a weight on top to flatten it out.

CITRUS PEEL CANDLES

You can add citrus cut-outs to all types of candles.

Fill a jar with dried orange slices and cranberries, tie on a homespun bow, attach citrus cut-outs and top with a flowerpot votive.

Knot a strip of homespun around a square pillar candle, add a citrus cut-out and place it on a tart tin filled with dried rose hips.

Fill a glass votive holder with crushed quince and a candle, then hang citrus cut-outs from the top of the holder.

Create orange peel ornaments by peeling the orange in sections as large as possible. Cut in ¼-inch wide strips and wrap tightly around a pencil; tape the ends. Leave on the pencil until dry (about 4 days or so). Glue on ribbon with glue gun or poke hole for string before drying. Gives a corkscrew effect and smells delicious!

Cover your pomanders with a rectangle of netting and close at the top with ribbons. Hang on your tree with a satin ribbon loop.

Tuck herb bundles in an evergreen tree along with small bunches of angel hair or baby's breath.

MASON JAR NATURALS

Fill jars with dried apple slices, pomegranates, cinnamon sticks or rose hips; place the lids on the jars. Tie a strip of homespun into a bow around each lid, then glue buttons and dried fruit slices to the bows.

For the kitchen, try rolling the Styrofoam balls in fragrant spices, dried beans, poppy or sesame seeds

QUICK & EASY POMANDERS

(MY VERY FAVORITE)

PUSH WHOLE CLOVES INTO A STYROFOAM BALL TO FORM A DESIGN.

FILL A PLASTIC BAG WITH GROUND NUTMEG & CINNAMON ~ SHAKE IT GENTLY TO MIX SPICES.

IN A SMALL DISH, ADD A FEW DROPS OF SPICY CITRUS OIL TO WHITE GLUE, AND BRUSH IT ON THE CLOVE-STUDDED BALL.

DROP GLUEY BALL INTO SPICE BAG ~ don't let the ball touch the sides of the bag! ~AND SHAKE GENTLY 'TIL BALL IS COVERED.

ALLOW TO DRY.

PUT 'EM IN A BOWL WITH HOLLY & PINECONES.

Fill a bowl with fragrant pomanders, then tie a big fabric bow around the bowl…top the bow with a button.

PAPER EDGINGS

Make paper edgings for every shelf, mantel or doorway of the house. Trace one of the patterns, page 143, onto tracing paper and cut out. Fold your paper accordion-style using the width indicated on the pattern. Draw around the pattern on folded paper, then use sharp straight or decorative-edge scissors to cut out the shape…try using a tiny hole punch or a push pin to add some details…unfold and voilá!…a whole bunch of shapes. Tape several edgings together to form a long chain. For larger paper edgings, use newspaper, grocery bags or wrapping paper and enlarge the patterns on a photocopy machine.

Get out your paper and scissors and get ready to trim more than the tree! These festive shelf edgings shaped like snowmen, icicles, hearts and angels are so fun to make…your whole family will want to help.

Have the kids make paper snowflakes for Grandma and Grandpa, or far-away relatives. They're so easy to mail, and a treat to receive! They're also great to mail to our servicemen and women spending the holidays away from home. Check with your local government office for a listing of addresses.

CUTe as A ButtOn

So many buttons…"sew" many ideas!
Here are lots of clever ways to use your fabric
scraps and old button collections to create
the season's folkiest holiday treasures.

This Tree-Topper Star rises to the occasion. Use your choice of homespun fabrics and buttons to create your own unique
design, then stuff with polyester fiberfill! Instructions are on page 126.

STOCKING ORNAMENTS, STAR ORNAMENTS, WREATH ORNAMENTS AND BOW GARLAND

Whether for your tree or packages, homespun ornaments and garland add an old-fashioned touch to your holidays. For stockings, embellish miniature socks with fabric and buttons. For wreath and star ornaments, use the patterns on page 133 to shape a length of heavy craft wire. Wrap the shape with strips of homespun...add a loop for hanger, then glue on lots of buttons. For the garland, tie 1"x4" strips of fabric to a piece of jute...keep tying until you have your desired length, then glue on buttons.

For an old-fashioned country Christmas, drape a quilt around the base of your tree instead of a tree skirt.

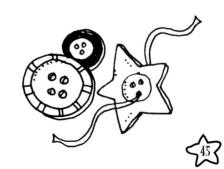

Your appliquéd Button Tree Skirt will be one-of-a-kind when you follow your heart to select your favorite fabrics and buttons. Instructions are on page 126.

46

Visit your local office supply store for a stack of small manilla envelopes.

Kate ♥

Put a gift certificate or a wish for the coming year inside the envelope, seal it and glue on a neat button. Sew a thread loop on the envelope and hang it on the tree... make one for everybody!

Hot-glue tiny buttons on clear glass Christmas tree balls... tie on a homespun rag ribbon... quick & easy!

Decorate your halls, walls and other areas with miniature Stocking Ornaments, Star Ornaments, and a homespun Bow Garland crafted with strips of old-fashioned fabrics and assorted buttons! Find the instructions on page 45.

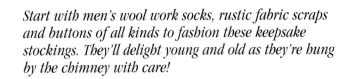

Start with men's wool work socks, rustic fabric scraps and buttons of all kinds to fashion these keepsake stockings. They'll delight young and old as they're hung by the chimney with care!

PRIMITIVE STOCKINGS

Bring new life to your lost mate or gently worn socks. Follow your Country Friends® technique for *Coffee or Tea Dyeing*, page 130, to dye your socks. Tear patches and cut shapes from fabric scraps...add a heel or toe if you'd like. Using 6 strands of floss and primitive stitches, arrange and stitch patches, shapes and assorted buttons on stockings...be careful, you only want to stitch through the front of the stockings. Fold a length of jute in half and sew ends to the inside top of stockings for a hanger. As easy as these are, you can make stockings for everyone!

*C*reate ribbons and bows from your favorite country fabric by cutting or tearing it into strips. It's less expensive than yards of ribbon. One square yard of fabric will provide lots of strips, which are pretty tied on wreaths, packages or around doorknobs.

Decorate a tiny artificial tree with old buttons. Tie them on with embroidery floss. Wrap the base of the tree in a piece of homespun and tie with jute. Perfect for the sewing room!

Bring out all your very best quilts and layer in chairs, couches, fold on top of cupboards...make your home cozy for the holidays!

BUTTON LAMP

- fabrics for lampshade and top and bottom trim
- 4"x11"x6" self-adhesive lampshade
- paper-backed fusible web
- yellow and green felt
- yellow and black embroidery floss
- assorted buttons
- hot glue gun
- pinking shears
- quart-size jar with lid
- jar lamp wiring kit
- quart-size wire jar holder

Refer to Embroidery Stitches, page 130, before beginning project. Use 6 strands of floss for all embroidery stitches.

1. Follow manufacturer's instructions to cut fabric to cover shade.

2. Using patterns, page 140, follow *Making Appliqués*, page 130, to make one tree appliqué from green felt and 4 star appliqués from yellow felt.

(continued on page 127)

Teeny Tiny old time Stockings

You'll need:

- ◆ 4 Teabags
- ◆ 2 pairs red or green tiny baby socks, prewashed
- ◆ paper towels
- ◆ buttons
- ◆ embroidery floss

. . . .

1. Prepare some strong hot tea with the teabags in a bowl full of hot water. Let tea cool slightly.

2. Add socks one·by·one to the tea ~ let sit for 2 to 4 minutes. Tea will stain socks for an antiqued look.

3. Remove socks ~ blot dry with layers of paper towels. Lay socks on towels to dry.

4. Fold down top of each sock to form a cuff.

5. Stitch on buttons around cuff with embroidery floss.

Ideas! Raid your button box for neat <u>old</u> buttons, or buy new alphabet-letter buttons to spell out a name... Fill with tiny candy and use as a "place card"... make these using little mittens, too!

Organize your family photographs in an album with lots of personality! Ours is covered with homespun and decorated with a favorite picture and a buttoned-up mat. See page 127 for instructions.

Festive Little Touches

A heartwarming snowman here, a peaceful angel there...these are the little touches that make your home glow with holiday cheer.

SNOWMAN JAR

Refer to our Country Friends® *Painting Techniques*, page 131, for some painting tips to use while making your Snowman Jar. *Sponge Paint* a white snowman with a black hat on an ordinary jar...add a hand-painted nose, eyes, mouth, buttons and a few snowflakes drifting around the snowman. Lightly mist snowman with wood-tone spray...*Spatter Paint* the jar white.

Twist a length of craft wire around the top of the jar...curl the ends. Glue a miniature snowflake from your Snowflake Garden, page 24, to each end of the wire. Tie several strands of raffia into a bow around the top of the jar, covering the wire. Glue a holly sprig to the knot of the bow. Light a candle in the jar, then relax and let the soft, warm glow of the candlelight take you back to "I remember when...".

Topped off with a raffia bow and a sprig of greenery, this sponge-painted Snowman Jar will make the season bright.

NATURAL ANGELS

- white felt
- polyester fiberfill
- 4-inch tall wooden doll clothespin
- country print fabric
- hot glue gun
- dried bay leaves
- dried apple slices

1. For each angel, cut one 2½-inch square from felt. Place a small amount of fiberfill at center of felt square. Gather felt around top of clothespin; wrap and tie thread around gathers to secure.

2. Tear a 3½"x9" piece from fabric for dress. Work Running Stitches, page 130, along one long edge of dress. Pull ends of thread to gather dress around neck of angel; tie thread to secure.

3. Glue 2 bay leaves to angel for wings and an apple slice over bay leaves for halo.

Beautiful Christmas Decorations From the Grocery Store?

It's true! Push your shopping cart down the produce aisle for gorgeous, natural decorations this holiday season:

JUST LOOK AT ALL THE LOVELY SHADES OF RED IN THE <u>APPLE</u> BINS! A PILE OF BRIGHT & SHINY JONATHANS IN A BIG WOODEN BOWL SAYS COUNTRY CHRISTMAS... HOLLOW OUT RED & GREEN APPLES AND FILL WITH TEA-LIGHTS TO MARCH ACROSS A WINDOWSILL OR MANTEL.

A TALL GLASS CYLINDER OR VASE SHOWS OFF THE BEAUTY OF <u>WALNUTS OR PECANS</u> IN THE SHELL. TIE A FEW STRANDS OF RAFFIA 'ROUND IT AND TUCK IN A SPRIG OF EVERGREEN. FIX SEVERAL DIFFERENT CONTAINERS, EACH WITH A DIFFERENT KIND OF NUT INSIDE, AND DISPLAY THEM TOGETHER FOR AN INTERESTING LOOK.

A CRYSTAL COMPOTE OR CAKE PLATE LAYERED WITH <u>CRANBERRIES</u> IS BEAUTIFUL WHEN YOU "PLANT" A WHITE PILLAR CANDLE IN THEIR MIDST.

More To Try:

★ A bunch of <u>carrots</u> tied up with a christmas ribbon for you-know-who!

★ A pyramid of <u>oranges</u> on a white ironstone platter with greenery sprigs tucked 'round the base.

Choose a Christmasy plaid ribbon and make dozens of bows for accents around the house. Use them on the tree and for wreaths, along with cedar roping inside and out. You can even use the same ribbon to tie up bundles of greens, dried flowers and dried berries to hang over doorways.

Frosty Winter Windows

Dab water-soluble paint over decorative paper doilies on each windowpane...the snowflake designs wipe off easily with a damp sponge! You can also add wintry snowflakes to mirrors and car windows, too.

PAINTED GLASS ORNAMENTS

Nothing says Christmas like treasured ornaments...especially when they're handmade. In no time at all, you can have a crate full of these ready to give to your special friends. Spray frosted glass ornaments with a light coat of wood-tone spray, then use dimensional paint to add the tree design...remember to let each color of paint dry before adding the next.

Candy Cane Vases: Attach candy canes (approximately 24, 5¹/₂-inch ones) to empty soup cans (label removed) with a hot glue gun. Do not remove cellophane wrappers; they will help prevent damage and protect candy from water. Tie a ribbon around the middle. Use as a vase for holly…or fill with soil and plant a paperwhite narcissus bulb (4 to 6 weeks before Christmas). Makes a nice hostess gift.

An idea if you have a large collection of Santas would be to have an "Advent Santa." Put a new one out each day until the REAL Santa comes.

OLD-FASHIONED SPOOL CANDLEHOLDERS

Here's an easy way to add a cozy, heartwarming touch to your home this holiday season! Search through antique shops, flea markets or Grandma's attic for old-fashioned wooden spools. Glue strips of fabric around the spindles of the spools. Add painted wooden cut-outs, raffia bows, assorted buttons, torn fabric bows, moss or artificial greenery for embellishment. Top each spool with a coordinating taper or pillar candle.

Does your tree look "lonely" before and after the presents? Arrange your children's stuffed animals or dolls to sit beneath it until the packages arrive or you take down the tree.

JOY

Fill crockery bowls with scented pinecones & apples.

Line cupboard shelves with bright holiday plaid towels.

Tie a dogbone wreath over Spot's dish.

STARS

Beads

Extra Roping

55

Heart · Felt and ♥ Hand · made

The best-loved and most-remembered gifts of the season are handmade. For kids, turn a plain muslin doll into Raggedy Suzanne, or make a gingerboy from work socks. For grown-ups, put together homespun reindeer pins with jute antlers and red jingle bell noses. Don't forget Mary Elizabeth's ideas for snuggly fleece throws, too! Craft a candle in a clay pot, a potpourri-packed Shaker box with a painted snowman and many more gifts! Wrap 'em in plain brown paper and adorn with lots of greenery and naturals!

Brown paper packages decorated with homespun strips and lots of naturals, greenery and berries are simply elegant...and so simple! Let our packages and baskets inspire you, then collect your favorite naturals and start gluing.

Kate's ☆ bright and shiny Word ☆ Wrap

noel

☆ ☆

snowflakes

☆

mittens

peace on earth

oh joy

☆

berry

stars & snowy skies

candy canes

☆

merry

christmas

oh joy

Do something extraordinary! Wrap a few packages in solid-color paper, then use a paint pen to hand-letter your favorite words or symbols of the season. Use your imagination!

STENCILS & RIBBONS & OLD BUTTONS & HOMESPUN IDEAS....

snowflake wrapping paper

Plastic snowflakes make great stencils for gift wrap. Place the snowflakes on the paper and lightly spray them with spray paint. Move the stencils and keep going until you have enough paper to cover your package...don't forget an extra square for a gift tag.

The Kids Will Love 'em!

Choose Christmasy plaids and stripes to dress up a plain muslin doll as Raggedy Suzanne, then create a soft, huggable gingerboy using country-style work socks. Instructions begin on page 127.

CANDY CANE PILLOWCASE

Cut a 1³/4-inch and a 2¹/4-inch wide strip from fabrics to fit around the open end of a pillowcase. Press the long edges of each strip ¹/2-inch to the wrong side…fuse ³/4-inch wide web tape to the back of each strip. Arrange and fuse strips around pillowcase…you can sew the edges of the strips in place to make them more durable. Use the pattern, page 142, and follow *Making Appliqués*, page 131, to make 6 candy cane appliqués from fabric. Arrange and fuse the candy canes on pillowcase, then sew buttons to the pillowcase as desired.

*E*ager little ones always want to open gifts early, so this year start your own "Twelve Days of Christmas." In each Christmas stocking, place twelve stocking stuffers. Start on December 13th and, each morning, let them open one stocking stuffer. The last one is opened on Christmas Eve, and Christmas Day is then left to open all the gifts under the tree!

HANDY RANDY REINDEER

THE KIDS WILL MAKE A WHOLE HERD!

- LIGHT BROWN CONSTRUCTION PAPER
- DARK BROWN CONSTRUCTION PAPER
- RED CONSTRUCTION PAPER OR A POMPOM FOR THE NOSE
- PLASTIC WIGGLY EYES
- WHITE GLUE

1. TRACE AROUND CHILD'S FOOT ON LIGHT BROWN PAPER TO MAKE REINDEER HEAD. CUT OUT.

2. ON DARK BROWN PAPER, TRACE AROUND CHILD'S HANDS TO MAKE REINDEER ANTLERS. CUT OUT.

3. GLUE ON RED CONSTRUCTION PAPER CIRCLE OR POMPOM FOR NOSE. GLUE ON TWO WIGGLY EYES.

4. DECORATE BEDROOM DOORS WITH A HERD OF RANDYS & GREEN CONSTRUCTION PAPER TREES!

Warm and Wonderful

Gift-giving is "sew" wonderful when you can transform ordinary thermal shirts into one-of-a-kind originals. Our blanket-stitched fabric appliqués add lots of whimsical charm.

PRIMITIVE REINDEER PIN

Cut 3 inches from the toe-end of a child-size sock; discard cuff. With the open end at top, sew on a jingle bell for a nose and black beads for eyes. Use black floss to make several *Straight Stitches*, page 130, for a mouth and one above each eye for eyebrows. Lightly stuff the head with fiberfill.

For each antler, knot a 4-inch length of jute at the center. Place one end of each antler in top of head. Stitch antlers in place and sew opening closed; unravel antlers.

For the bow tie, knot a torn ³/₄"x4" fabric strip at center. Sew the bow tie and a button on the reindeer. Sew a pin back to the back of the reindeer.

APPLIQUÉD THERMAL SHIRTS

Warm and cozy, these thermal shirts make great gifts for friends and family. Use the patterns, page 144 or 145, and follow *Making Appliqués*, page 131, to make the appliqués from fabrics. Fuse the appliqués in place and use *Blanket Stitches*, page 130, to secure them on the shirt. Add some festive bias trim around the neck and cuffs…holiday wear in a jiffy!

REINDEER SWEATSHIRT

Dress the kids for Santa's visit in this sweatshirt appliquéd with some of his playful reindeer in training, Fun, Frolic & Whimsy! Use the patterns on page 139 and follow *Making Appliqués*, page 131, to make desired number of reindeer appliqués from felt. Arrange and fuse the appliqués on a sweatshirt. Use brown floss to sew on beads for noses, make *Straight Stitches*, page 130, for antlers and make *Lazy Daisy Stitches*, page 130, for tails. Catching bells in stitching, use green floss to make *Straight Stitches* along neck seam.

A loving gift for your child that's straight from the heart…assemble a recipe box with all Grandma's and Mom's family recipes. Add new recipes each year along with funny little notes and sayings. A warm, wonderful gift to grow right along with your child…truly a box full of memories!

Mary Elizabeth's
Cozy Christmas
Fleece Ideas

Toasty & Terrific Scarves

Mary Elizabeth makes one for all of her friends...
after all, every neck needs one!

- 1 yd. polar fleece (makes three 12"x60" scarves)
- needle
- scraps of felt
- embroidery floss
- buttons

STEP 1. Cut fleece into 3 strips (width-wise).

STEP 2. Make one-inch-long clips in each end for fringe.

STEP 3. Cut out stars & squares from felt... the patterns are on page 146. Pin them to one end of the scarf.

STEP 4. Work Blanket Stitches, page 130, around the inner squares and Running Stitches, page 130, around the stars... add buttons.

★ design ideas: blue fleece with yellow stars & moon ....red scarf with green trees & brown buttons ....

A heartwarming gift, this scarf and mitten set is simple to make with polar fleece, scraps of felt and buttons from your craft basket! See page 128 for the mitten instructions.

Soft & Snuggly Throws

... your friends will be snug as a bug in a rug if you give these for gifts!

· · · · · · · ·

- 1½ yard polar fleece (this will make one 54"x58" throw)
- cotton yarn in contrasting color
- needle (with eye large enough for yarn)
- embroidery floss
- felt & fabric

STeP 1. Using Blanket Stitches, page 130, hand-stitch all the way around the polar fleece edge with yarn.

STeP 2. Add the felt & fabric designs...the patterns are on pages 148-151. Use floss & Embroidery Stitches, page 130, to sew them in place. Add buttons and any other accents you like.

Snuggle up with your little ones under a warm cozy blanket and watch the snow fall.

JUST·a·THOUGHT:

- Make smaller versions of the throws for the kids & babies in your family.

- You might like to decorate a corner of each throw with a felt design, too ～ just like Mary Elizabeth's scarves.

- Dig around in your button basket for interesting & beautiful buttons to sew on each project.

¡Fleece Navidad!

Our warm fleece throws have homespun appliqués to please Mom, Dad or the kids!

67

and precious are all things that come from
FRIENDS
~Theocritus

Christmas is a joyous time when lasting friendships are celebrated and handmade gifts are cheerfully exchanged. Kindness is the order of the day!

Charmingly embroidered in schoolgirl style, this framed friendship verse is sweetened by appliquéd hearts and a border of colorful fabric strips and buttons! The simple instructions are on page 128.

PEPPERBERRY CANDLEHOLDER

Fill a flowerpot with sand. Secure a pillar candle in the pot. Arrange and glue boxwood, then pepperberries around the rim of the pot.

Great fillers for gift baskets are sachets, potpourris, candles, ornaments, cookie cutters, tiny boxed candies, teas, cinnamon sticks, spices, sugar shakers, wooden spoons, kitchen gadgets, homespun towels, seeds, fragrant soaps, bubble bath, gourmet jams, jellies, etc.

Mix potpourri, hard candies or sprigs of fragrant greenery with packing materials when preparing a gift for shipping. It adds a festive and aromatic touch for the recipient.

"The best gifts are tied with heartstrings."
— Anonymous

It is a good thing to be rich, and a good thing to be strong, but it is a better thing to be loved of many friends.
~EURIPIDES~

*Paint a cool snowman on a wooden Shaker box
and pack it with fragrant potpourri. Our easy
instructions are on page 129.*

FRIENDSHIP FRAME

Spray paint a wooden frame red...lightly
spray it with wood-tone spray. Trace the
friendship design, page 154, onto tracing
paper, then use transfer paper to
transfer the design to the frame. Draw
over the design with a black paint pen.
Glue torn one inch wide strips of fabric
along the sides and bottom of
frame...add a bow at the top and
buttons at each corner.

I'm so glad we're Friends.

Wrap gifts as you purchase them. Then there's no mad rush wrapping so many at once.

SACHET PILLOWS

Using one of the patterns from pages 153-155 and pinking shears, cut 2 of the same shape from red felt for each sachet...the star has a middle white layer cut ¼-inch larger than the pattern. Trace the greenery design onto tracing paper, pin the tracing paper to the front of one shape, then work *Straight Stitches*, page 130, over the design...carefully tear away the paper. Sew buttons over the design. Pin your shapes together and work *Running Stitches*, page 130, along edges to secure...before you completely sew it together, stuff with your favorite scent of potpourri, then finish sewing closed. For the "purse" sachet, fold down the flap, then sew on a big button to secure.

GIFTS that TASTE GOOD

When Christmas rolls around, the Country Friends® love to share homemade treats from the kitchen! Mary Elizabeth enjoys preparing melt-in-your-mouth cookies and confections. Holly likes to help out busy families with quick-to-fix meals, and you can always count on something chocolate from Kate! Turn the page to discover scrumptious goodies, along with ideas for creative packaging...and enjoy your gifts of good taste!

Cookies, cookies, cookies! No one can resist these delicious favorites, and decorated cookie jars add to the fun. Look on page 74 for the recipes and page 129 to find instructions for the jars.

OLD-FASHIONED ICED SUGAR COOKIES
These cookies will make memories for years to come.

2 c. vegetable shortening
2 1/2 c. sugar
1 1/2 t. orange zest, grated
1 1/2 t. vanilla extract
3 eggs
1/4 c. orange juice
6 c. all-purpose flour
4 1/2 t. baking powder
3/4 t. salt

Cream together shortening, sugar, orange zest and vanilla. Add eggs to creamed mixture; mix well. Add orange juice and mix. Sift flour, baking powder and salt; add to creamed mixture and blend. Chill for 2 hours, covered. Once chilled, roll dough 1/8 to 1/4-inch thick on lightly floured surface. Cut out with favorite cutters. Use floured spatula to pick up cut-out cookies and put on ungreased cookie sheet. Bake at 375 degrees for 7 to 10 minutes. Cool before removing from cookie sheet; ice when cool.

Royal Icing:
3 1/4 c. powdered sugar
5 T. water
2 1/2 T. meringue powder

Beat powdered sugar, water and meringue powder in a medium bowl at high speed of an electric mixer 7 to 10 minutes or until stiff. Ice cookies and let dry. Once dry, layer cookies in boxes or tins with wax paper between each layer.

Lori Goodell
Lancaster, CA

Warm cookies dipped in cold milk...one of life's simple pleasures.

BROWN SUGAR SPICE COOKIES
They are so delicious, no icing is needed.

1 1/2 c. butter, softened
2 c. brown sugar, packed
1 egg
4 c. all-purpose flour
2 t. cinnamon
1 t. nutmeg
1/2 t. cloves
1/4 t. baking soda

Cream butter and brown sugar; add egg. Beat until light and fluffy. Stir flour with spices and baking soda; add to creamed mixture. Mix well. Cover and chill until firm, about 2 hours. On floured surface, roll dough to 1/8-inch thickness. Cut into shapes with cookie cutters. Place on ungreased cookie sheet. Bake at 350 degrees for 8 to 10 minutes or until lightly browned. Makes 6 dozen cookies.

Sandra Bowman

LEMON-BASIL COOKIES
A good lemony cookie!

1/4 c. butter, softened
8-oz. pkg. cream cheese, softened
1 egg yolk
1 t. lemon juice
18 1/4-oz. box lemon cake mix
1/4 c. coconut, shredded
1/4 c. walnuts, chopped
1 T. dried basil
1/2 t. lemon zest, grated

Cream butter and cream cheese. Add egg yolk and lemon juice; stir until blended. Blend in dry cake mix one-third at a time, last portion by hand. Stir in the coconut, nuts, basil and lemon zest. Drop by teaspoonfuls onto a greased cookie sheet and flatten with a glass dipped in sugar. Bake at 350 degrees for 10 to 15 minutes or until golden in color.

Elizabeth Timmins
Gooseberry Patch

CHERRY & PECAN COOKIES
A tasty combination of flavors.

1 c. vegetable shortening
2 c. brown sugar, packed
2 eggs
1/2 c. water
3 1/2 c. all-purpose flour
1 t. baking soda
1 t. salt
1 1/2 c. pecans, chopped
2 c. maraschino cherries, sliced

Mix all ingredients together. Chill at least one hour. Drop by teaspoonfuls onto cookie sheet. Bake at 400 degrees for 8 to 10 minutes. Makes 8 dozen.

Cathy Twohig
Centerville, VA

MOCHA TRUFFLE COOKIES
A rich coffee-flavored chocolate cookie.

1/2 c. butter or margarine
1 1/2 c. semi-sweet chocolate chips, divided
1 T. instant coffee crystals
3/4 c. sugar
3/4 c. brown sugar, packed
2 eggs
2 t. vanilla extract
2 c. all-purpose flour
1/3 c. cocoa
1/2 t. baking powder
1/4 t. salt

In a large saucepan, melt butter and 1/2 cup chocolate chips over low heat. Remove from heat. Stir in coffee crystals. Cool for 5 minutes. Stir in sugars, eggs and vanilla. In a medium mixing bowl, combine flour, cocoa, baking powder and salt. Stir into coffee mixture. Stir in the remaining one cup chocolate chips. Drop by tablespoonfuls onto greased cookie sheets. Bake at 350 degrees for 10 minutes.

Bernice Ladroot

YOU'RE AN Angel!!

HEAVENLY MACAROONS
So quick and easy...coco-nutty!

1¹/₃ c. flaked coconut
¹/₂ t. vanilla extract
¹/₃ c. sweetened condensed
    milk

Combine all ingredients, mixing well.
Drop by teaspoonfuls one inch
apart onto well-greased cookie
sheet. Bake at 350 degrees for
10 to 12 minutes or until golden
brown. Remove at once from cookie
sheet. To make chocolate
macaroons, fold in melted one-ounce
square semi-sweet chocolate
before baking. Makes approximately
2 dozen.

Jeannine English
Wylie, TX

CHOCOLATE COFFEE
A quick and easy mix to keep on hand.

¹/₂ c. instant coffee crystals
1¹/₂ c. powdered creamer
¹/₂ c. chocolate-flavored
    powdered drink mix
¹/₄ c. sugar
¹/₈ t. salt
¹/₂ t. nutmeg

Mix ingredients together in a
blender. Add to cup of hot water
according to taste.

Betty Sack

For that friend who's been there through thick and thin, pack a bag of
Heavenly Macaroons! Turn to page 53 to make the country angel...
simply photocopy the tag design on page 156 and cut out.

*aaahh...
that's good!*

Chill-chaser

First, gather up the ingredients:

½ c. dried pinto beans
½ c. dried kidney beans
2 T. dried minced onion

1 T. dried pepper flakes
½ t. dried minced garlic

Rinse and sort through beans and discard any shriveled ones. Spread out on a paper towel to dry overnight. Combine with the other ingredients above and package in a cello bag or mason jar.

★

Now, make the Seasoning Packet:

1½ t. paprika
1 t. cumin
1 t. chili powder
1 t. oregano

½ t. turmeric
½ t. black pepper
¼ t. red pepper
⅛ t. cayenne pepper

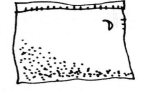

Combine all these spices together and package in a plastic bag.

★

Tie the whole thing (card, jar & bag) together with raffia and a dried chili pepper.

Turn a knitted stocking cap upside down, and put the chili fixings (jar, baggie, recipe card) inside...maybe even put the seasoning packet into mittens first! Tie shut with red yarn.

Chili

WARM UP!

Chill-chaser chili

1 Pkg. bean mix
1 lb. lean ground beef
1/4 c. onion, chopped
1/4 c. green pepper, chopped
28 oz. can stewed tomatoes
Seasoning packet
1 to 2 c. water (as needed)

Deliver the fixings for Chill-Chaser Chili in a brown paper lunch bag that you paint with a frosty snowman. For the recipe card, paint the same snowman on kraft paper; photocopy the recipe on page 156 and glue everything to an index card.

For the super snackers on your list, bake up batches of crunchy munchies! Page 129 tells how to transform "recycled" coffee and soup cans into creative gift canisters.

CARAMEL PRETZELS & NUTS

A sweet glaze coats these pretzels and peanuts.

16 c. sm. pretzel twists
2 c. roasted peanuts
2 c. brown sugar, packed
1/4 c. light corn syrup
1/4 c. molasses
1 t. salt
1 t. baking soda
1 t. almond extract

Place pretzels and peanuts in a 20"x14" oven cooking bag sprayed with cooking spray. In a 2-quart microwave-safe bowl, combine sugar, corn syrup and molasses. Microwave on high power (100%) 2 minutes or until mixture boils. Stir and microwave 2 minutes longer. Stir in salt, baking soda and almond extract. Pour syrup over pretzel mixture; stir and shake until well coated. Microwave 1 1/2 minutes on high. Stir, shake and microwave 1 1/2 minutes longer. Spread on greased aluminum foil. Cool. Store in an airtight container. Makes about 22 cups.

SUGARED NUTS

Caution! These could be addictive.

1 egg white
1/2 c. sugar
1/2 t. cinnamon
2 11-oz. cans lightly salted
   mixed nuts

Beat egg white until foamy. Stir in sugar, cinnamon and nuts, coating nuts well. Spread on a greased baking sheet. Bake at 225 degrees for one hour, stirring every 15 minutes. Cool. Store in an airtight container. Makes about 6 cups.

CURRY CHEESE SNACKS

Just the right amount of curry gives this snack a rich flavor.

9 c. sm. pretzel twists
2 c. square corn cereal
2 c. square rice cereal
1 c. roasted peanuts
1 c. margarine, melted
3 1 1/4-oz. pkgs. cheese sauce
   mix
1 1/2 t. curry powder

Place pretzels, cereals and peanuts in a large bowl. Combine remaining ingredients; pour over pretzel mixture. Stir until well coated. Spread on 2 ungreased baking sheets. Bake at 350 degrees for 8 to 10 minutes or until lightly browned, stirring twice. Cool on paper towels. Store in an airtight container. Makes about 12 1/2 cups.

Get your friends together for a night of baking and cookie decorating. Give your finished goodies to the fire or police department staffs who have to work Christmas Day.

Keep an eye out for garage sale treasures...gift canisters, pretty mismatched plates, etc...great for delivering food gifts!

CRUNCHY CARAMEL SNACK MIX

Sweet and crunchy...a wonderful combination!

3 c. chocolate puffed corn
   cereal
3 c. bite-size square oat cereal
2 c. sm. pretzel twists
1 c. unsalted peanuts
1 c. brown sugar, packed
1/2 c. margarine
1/4 c. light corn syrup
1/4 t. baking soda
1/4 t. cream of tartar
1/2 t. vanilla extract

In a 13"x9" pan, combine cereals, pretzels and peanuts; set aside. Combine brown sugar, margarine and corn syrup. Cook and stir over medium heat until margarine melts and mixture comes to a boil. Cook without stirring for 4 minutes. Remove from heat; stir in baking soda and cream of tartar. Stir in vanilla. Pour over cereal mixture. Bake at 300 degrees for 30 minutes, stirring after 15 minutes. Transfer to large shallow pan. Cool. Store in an airtight container. Makes 10 cups.

Kathy Bolyea
Naples, FL

WHO CAN BEAR TO WAIT FOR 'EM TO COME OUT OF THE OVEN?

LAYERED OATMEAL-CHIP COOKIE MIX

Hand writing the instruction card gives this gift a special touch. Decorate it with holiday stickers or rubber stamps, too.

½ c. sugar
½ c. brown sugar, packed
1 c. quick-cooking oats
1 c. crispy rice cereal
½ c. chocolate chips
1 c. all-purpose flour
½ t. salt
½ t. baking powder

Layer first 5 ingredients in order listed, in a one-quart, wide-mouth glass canning jar. Press down firmly on each layer before adding the next ingredient. Combine flour, salt and baking powder together, mixing well. Add flour mixture on top of the chocolate chip layer. Add a gift card with the following instructions: Mix the jar of ingredients with ½ cup softened margarine, one beaten egg and one teaspoon vanilla extract, blending well. Shape into one-inch balls and place 2 inches apart on an ungreased cookie sheet. Bake at 350 degrees for 10 minutes. Makes 4 dozen cookies.

Virginia Graybill
Hershey, PA

Surprise a busy baker with a jar of Layered Oatmeal-Chip Cookie Mix! It looks pretty and the cookies are yummy. Top the jar with a circle of fabric and write the baking instructions on a festive recipe card.

PUMPKIN BUTTER

Microwave easy!

15-oz. can pumpkin
3 T. powdered pectin
1 t. cinnamon
½ t. allspice
2¼ c. sugar

In a 2-quart microwave bowl, combine pumpkin, pectin, cinnamon and allspice. Mix well. Microwave on high for 6 minutes or until very hot, mixing every 2 minutes. Add sugar; mix well. Microwave on high for 5 to 10 minutes or until full rolling boil, stirring once during cooking. Continue to boil for one minute. Spoon into 3 sterilized 8-ounce jars. Screw lids tight. Store in refrigerator up to 3 weeks or freeze up to 3 months.

Kathy Bolyea
Naples, FL

RAISIN SAUCE FOR CHRISTMAS HAM

Delicious served with sweet potatoes and applesauce.

¾ c. raisins
1 c. water
4 or 5 whole cloves
¾ c. brown sugar, not packed
1 t. cornstarch
¼ t. salt
¼ t. pepper
1 T. butter or margarine
1 T. lemon juice
¼ t. Worcestershire sauce

Cover raisins with water, add cloves and simmer for 10 minutes. Mix sugar, cornstarch, salt and pepper; add to raisin mixture. Stir until thickened over low heat. Add butter, lemon juice and Worcestershire sauce, stirring until thoroughly combined. Simmer a few minutes. Baste ham with mixture while baking.

Judy Hand
Centre Hall, PA

QUICK BREAD & BUTTER PICKLES

This recipe gets a blue ribbon for homemade taste without the fuss!

1-qt. jar whole kosher dill pickles, store-bought
1¹/2 c. sugar
1 onion, sliced
2 cinnamon sticks
2 T. vinegar

Drain pickles and cut into chunks ¹/2 to one-inch thick; place in clean jar. Combine sugar, onion, cinnamon sticks and vinegar; pour over pickles. Cover and refrigerate. Stir mixture once a day for 2 to 3 days. Your "homemade" pickles are ready to serve after 3 or 4 days.

HOT PEPPER JELLY

This looks "holiday special" and it tastes so good. Pack it with a wooden serving spoon. It's great with cream cheese and unsalted crackers.

1¹/2 c. green pepper, seeded and chopped
4-oz. can green chilies, drained
6¹/2 c. sugar
1¹/2 c. cider vinegar
¹/8 t. green food coloring
2 3-oz. pouches liquid fruit pectin

Put pepper and chilies in blender or food processor. Cover and process until puréed. In a stainless or enameled saucepan, heat sugar and vinegar until the sugar dissolves. Add pepper purée and bring to a boil over high heat. Reduce heat to moderately low and let simmer for 5 minutes. Stir in food coloring; skim off and discard foam. Remove from heat and stir in pectin. Pour into eight ¹/2-pint sterilized jars, filling each to within ¹/8-inch of the top. Seal jars with lids and screw bands or rubber rings and clamp tops. Cool upright on wire racks. Makes about eight ¹/2-pint jars.

Terrie Rasmussen
Sandy, UT

APPLE RELISH

Delicious served alongside baked ham or pork chops. No need to peel the apples…the skin adds a delicious crunch.

1 red cooking apple, chopped
1 green apple, chopped
¹/4 c. raisins
1 T. crystallized ginger, chopped
¹/2 c. onion, chopped
¹/4 c. sugar
¹/4 c. cider vinegar
¹/2 t. salt

In large saucepan, combine apples, raisins, ginger, onion, sugar, vinegar and salt. Heat until boiling, then reduce heat to low and simmer until onions are tender, about 5 to 7 minutes. Transfer to jars and cover tightly. Let cool to room temperature, then refrigerate.

ORANGE-CRANBERRY MARMALADE

Place in a vintage jar tied with a ribbon.

2 c. fresh cranberries
²/3 c. orange juice
2 t. orange zest, grated
¹/2 c. sugar

Place all ingredients in a 2-quart saucepan and bring to a boil over high heat. Reduce heat to low. Stirring occasionally, cover and simmer until cranberries pop and mixture thickens slightly, about 20 minutes. Store in refrigerator in a heat-proof jar. Makes 1¹/2 cups.

Terrie Rasmussen
Sandy, UT

The holidays are a great time to share the fruits of your summer canning! Decorate jars with fabric, ribbon or buttons; use colored pencils to hand-tint photocopies of the tags and labels on page 157.

CHOCOLATE CAPPUCCINO BROWNIES

Chewy and chocolatey together...delicious!

½ c. butter
1 c. brown sugar, packed
2 T. instant coffee crystals
3 eggs
1 t. vanilla extract
1 t. baking powder
½ t. salt
1¼ c. unbleached white flour, sifted
6 T. cocoa
½ c. brewed coffee, cooled
1 c. walnuts, chopped
1 c. semi-sweet chocolate chips

Melt the butter and add the brown sugar and coffee crystals; blend well. Add the eggs, vanilla, baking powder and salt and stir. Combine with flour, cocoa and coffee. Add nuts and chocolate chips. Pour batter into a 13"x9" pan and bake at 350 degrees for 25 to 30 minutes. Allow to cool and cut into squares. Makes 18 to 24.

MOM'S CURE-ALL SPICE TEA MIX

My mom, Helen Love, swears this tea cures colds!

1 c. powdered orange drink mix
⅔ c. dry instant tea
½ c. sugar
2 T. powdered lemonade mix
½ t. cinnamon
¼ t. cloves

Mix all ingredients together; place mix in container. To use, mix 2 teaspoons of mix per cup of boiling water.

Jeanne Elmer

HOLIDAY COCOA

A pair of mugs and a tin of holiday cookies would go nicely with this gift.

6 c. cocoa
2 c. malted milk powder
7 c. sugar
2 T. cinnamon
1 vanilla bean, split in half

Blend all ingredients and let sit for 3 days; remove vanilla bean. Spoon mixture into gift jars. Include these instructions with your gift: Mix ¼ cup of mix into an 8 to 10-ounce mug of hot milk.

Jacqueline Lash-Idler
Rockaway, NJ

There's nothing nicer on a frosty day than a cup of steaming cocoa! Tuck a bag of Holiday Cocoa mix and a pair of whimsical mugs in a basket, along with a set of cozy mitten coasters. Instructions for the coasters are on page 129.

TWO-TONE FUDGE
Two flavors...twice as delicious!

2 c. sugar
1 c. evaporated milk
14-oz. pkg. caramels
3/4 c. semi-sweet chocolate
    chips
1/2 c. peanut butter

Combine sugar and evaporated milk in 2-quart saucepan; add caramels. Place over low heat and cook, stirring constantly, until sugar is dissolved and mixture comes to a boil. Increase heat and boil for 4 minutes, stirring constantly. To 1½ cups of the mixture, add chocolate chips and stir until smooth. Pour into a greased 8"x8" pan. To remaining mixture, add peanut butter and stir until smooth. Pour into pan over chocolate mixture. Chill until firm and cut into squares. Yield: 2 lbs.

Karen Hayes

GARDEN HERB BREAD BLEND

1/3 c. dried parsley flakes
1/3 c. dried minced onions
2½ T. dried basil
2½ t. dried thyme leaves
2½ t. dried oregano leaves
1¼ t. garlic powder

Blend herbs together in bowl. Package in airtight container or bag. Makes one cup or enough for 6 loaves of bread.

Bread Recipe:
3 to 4 t. Garden Herb Bread
    Blend
1 pkg. hot roll mix
4 T. margarine, divided
1 egg

Add garden herb blend to dry hot roll mix. Follow instructions on hot roll mix box for mixing, kneading and resting. Shape dough into regular-size or mini loaves or follow instructions on box for rolls. Allow dough to rise. Bake regular-size bread loaves in greased loaf pans for 35 to 40 minutes at 375 degrees. Bake mini loaves about 10 minutes less, 25 to 30 minutes. Brush tops with remaining 2 tablespoons margarine.

BURGUNDY BEEF STEW
Fork-tender and richly flavored.

1½ lbs. boneless chuck, cubed
2 T. vegetable oil
2 baking potatoes, chopped
2 onions, peeled and chopped
4 carrots, chopped
1 turnip, chopped
3 T. all-purpose flour
1 c. beef broth
1 c. Burgundy wine
3 bay leaves
1 t. fresh basil, chopped
16-oz. can tomatoes, drained and
    chopped, optional

Brown the beef in hot vegetable oil in a large stew pot. Add all of the vegetables, except the tomatoes, and sauté over medium low for about 5 minutes. Sprinkle the flour over the meat and vegetables and stir to coat. Add broth, wine, seasonings and tomatoes. Bring to a boil and then reduce heat to low and simmer, covered, for 1½ hours or until meat is very tender, stirring occasionally.

"The best portion of a good man's life, his little, nameless, unremembered acts of kindness and love."
— William Wordsworth

Share the bounty of your summer herb garden with a packet of flavorful Garden Herb Bread Blend. Use colored pencils to tint a copy of the label design on page 156; give the mix and recipe along with a handy cutting board.

THE JOLLY CINNA-MEN
Everyone will love these!

2¼ c. brown sugar, packed
1 c. margarine, softened
3 eggs
4 c. all-purpose flour
1 t. baking soda
1 t. cinnamon

Cream sugar and margarine; add eggs and beat well. Add the rest of the ingredients; mix well and chill overnight. Roll out small amount of dough on floured board, keeping the rest of the dough refrigerated. If dough becomes too soft, put in freezer for a short time. Cut into desired shapes. Bake on greased cookie sheet at 350 degrees for 7 to 8 minutes.

Pat Ferrari
Sugarloaf, PA

Send a few tins of Christmas cookies to your local nursing home or hospital to brighten the season!

Volunteer to serve a holiday meal at your community shelter.

Treat someone to breakfast in bed…a pot of coffee or tea, freshly-baked muffins, the morning newspaper and a pretty flower.

The Jolly Cinna-Men will spread warm wishes! Decorate your basket with cheerful ribbon and a cookie cutter.

Vickie's Tea-Lover's Basket

Line a basket with paper doilies…add a tin of very special tea; homemade bread & preserves…a lacy napkin & beautiful antique china teacup…and a pretty jar of Vickie's lemon sugar.

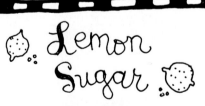

Lemon Sugar

1 c. sugar

1 pkg. (.23 oz) unsweetened lemonade-flavored soft drink mix

Combine well & place in jar

or cello bag tied tightly with ribbon.

WALNUT TEA LOAF
Not too sweet…moist and delicious.

1¹/3 c. honey
1¹/4 lbs. butter, melted and
    cooled
2 eggs
¹/2 c. whole milk
2 T. lemon juice
3¹/2 c. all-purpose flour
³/4 t. baking soda
1 t. cloves
¹/4 t. salt
1 c. walnuts, chopped
¹/2 c. raisins, optional

Combine honey, butter, eggs, milk and lemon juice until well blended. In a separate bowl, combine flour, baking soda, cloves and salt. Add flour mixture to the honey butter and beat until creamy. Fold in walnuts and raisins. Pour batter into 2 greased and floured 8¹/2"x4¹/2" loaf pans. Bake at 325 degrees for about one hour or until a toothpick comes out clean. Cool for 15 minutes, then turn onto racks to cool completely.

HOLIDAY GIFT CAKES
Make them as big or little as you want, and decorate accordingly. Wrap in brown paper tied with homespun or paper twist and a sprig of pine or holly.

8-oz. pkg. cream cheese,
    softened
1 c. margarine, softened
1¹/2 c. sugar
1¹/2 t. vanilla extract
4 eggs
2¹/4 c. sifted cake flour, divided
1¹/2 t. baking powder
8-oz. jar maraschino cherries,
    well drained and chopped
1 c. pecans, chopped and divided

Glaze:
1¹/2 c. powdered sugar, sifted
2 T. milk
Garnish: red or green maraschino
    cherry and pecan halves

Thoroughly blend cream cheese, margarine, sugar and vanilla. Add eggs, one at a time, mixing well after each addition. Sift 2 cups flour with baking powder. Gradually add sifted flour mixture to batter. Dredge cherries and ¹/2 cup pecans with remaining ¹/4 cup flour; fold into batter. Grease a 10-inch Bundt® or tube pan; sprinkle with ¹/2 cup finely chopped pecans. Pour batter into pan. Bake at 325 degrees for one hour and 20 minutes or until done. Cool 5 minutes; remove from pan. While cake is baking, prepare glaze; combine powdered sugar and milk. Add more milk, if needed, for drizzling consistency. Drizzle glaze over top and sides of cake. Garnish with cherry and pecan halves, as desired.
Yield: One 10-inch cake or 4 small loaves.

Judy Kelly
St. Charles, MO

Drizzle Holiday Gift Cakes with glaze, then decorate with festive cherry and pecan halves. Wrapping's a snap with kraft paper and a button-trimmed homespun bow. Finish with a hand-colored photocopy of the stocking tag design on page 156.

Savor the Flavor of Christmas

Like handmade gifts that touch the heart, the best-loved recipes we serve during the holidays are always eagerly anticipated. To ensure your Christmas fare leaves a lasting impression, the Country Friends® have whipped up some of their not-to-be-forgotten recipes! You'll find everything you need to plan a sit-down dinner, a drop-in open house, or a casual brunch. And there are plenty of goodies to satisfy everyone's sweet tooth, too!

Easy Plum Pudding is an after-dinner dish that will hit the spot. The no-fuss recipe can be found on page 118.

There is nothing greater than *SWEET ENTHUSIASM.*

*Who can resist the appeal of holiday goodies?
Delicious desserts, creative confections,
crispy cookies…we've got it all!*

NOEL ICE CREAM CUPS
A favorite with the kiddie crowd!

1 qt. vanilla ice cream, softened
1/4 c. pecans, toasted and
    chopped
2 T. red and green maraschino
    cherries, chopped
1 t. vanilla extract
1/2 t. almond extract
1/2 c. candy-coated chocolates,
    chopped

In a medium bowl, combine the ice cream, pecans, cherries and extracts, mixing well. Fold in candy-coated chocolates, reserving some for garnish. Spoon into paper-lined muffin cups and freeze for 30 minutes. Before serving, sprinkle with chopped candy-coated chocolates. Makes 8 to 10 servings.

Sue Major
Marblehead, OH

Noel Ice Cream Cups

WHITE CHOCOLATE CAKE

This triple-layer cake is elegant and different!

1 c. butter
2 c. sugar
4 eggs, beaten
4 oz. white chocolate, melted
2¹/₂ c. all-purpose flour
1 t. baking powder
1 t. vanilla extract
1 c. buttermilk
1 c. pecans or walnuts, chopped
1 c. flaked coconut

Cream butter and sugar with a mixer. Add eggs and melted chocolate, blending well. Add flour, baking powder, vanilla, buttermilk, chopped nuts and coconut. Blend well and pour into 3 prepared 9" round cake pans. Bake at 350 degrees about 35 minutes. Cool cake.

Icing:
¹/₂ c. butter or margarine, melted
4 oz. white chocolate
6 T. buttermilk
16-oz. box powdered sugar
1 t. vanilla extract

Mix butter, white chocolate and buttermilk together in a saucepan and heat gently, stirring until smooth. Remove from heat, add powdered sugar and vanilla and then return to heat to blend. Transfer icing to a medium bowl; chill 30 minutes, stirring every 10 minutes. Ice cake. Garnish with white or milk chocolate curls. For gift-giving, bake the cakes in mini-tube or Bundt® pans. Wrap each one in clear wrap and tie with ribbon.

*Judy Borecky
Escondido, CA*

White Chocolate Cake

APPLE CAKE WITH CINNAMON SAUCE

Try this with Gala or Jonathan apples for a change in taste.

1¹/₂ c. oil
2 c. sugar
4 eggs
2¹/₂ c. all-purpose flour
2 t. baking powder
1 t. cinnamon
3 c. Red Delicious apples, peeled and chopped
1 t. vanilla extract

Mix together oil and sugar. Beat in eggs one at a time. In a separate bowl, combine flour, baking powder and cinnamon; blend into egg mixture. Fold in apples and vanilla; mix thoroughly. Pour batter into an 8"x8" greased and floured cake pan. Bake at 350 degrees for 30 minutes. Cool, remove from pan and serve with Cinnamon Sauce.

Cinnamon Sauce:
2 c. water, boiling
2 c. brown sugar, packed
¹/₄ c. butter
¹/₄ c. all-purpose flour
2 t. vanilla extract
1¹/₂ t. cinnamon
1 t. salt

Combine all ingredients in a saucepan and bring to a boil, stirring constantly. Serve warm over slices of Apple Cake.

STEAMED CHOCOLATE PUDDING

Christmas day at my grandmother's and grandfather's house was always filled with family, presents, games and an ample mid-afternoon dinner. She made the pudding in an old fluted tin pudding mold. When she died, my mother gave the tin to me. It is one of my treasured possessions.

1 egg
1 c. sugar
2 T. butter, softened
2 oz. unsweetened
    chocolate, melted
1³/4 c. all-purpose flour, sifted
¹/2 t. salt
¹/4 t. cream of tartar
¹/4 t. baking soda
1 c. milk

Beat first 4 ingredients together, mixing well. Sift flour, salt, cream of tartar and soda together; combine with egg mixture. Slowly add in milk. Pour into a greased one-quart pudding mold. Cover with lid. Set mold on rack inside a Dutch oven. Add boiling water to come halfway up sides of mold. Cover and keep water at a gentle boil, adding boiling water as necessary. Steam for 3 hours or until a toothpick inserted in the center comes out clean. Serve with Hard Sauce.

Hard Sauce:
¹/3 c. butter, softened
1 c. powdered sugar
1 T. whipping cream
1 t. vanilla extract

Cream butter and gradually add in other ingredients; beat until fluffy. Chill until cold, but not hard. Yields ³/4 cup of sauce.

Nancy Campbell
Bellingham, WA

Steamed Chocolate Pudding

JUDY'S PRIZE-WINNING TOASTED PECAN CAKE

This local winner was featured on the front page of the San Diego newspaper.

1¹/3 c. pecans, chopped
¹/4 c. butter
3 c. all-purpose flour
2 t. baking powder
¹/2 t. salt
1 c. butter, softened
2 c. sugar
4 eggs
1 c. milk
2 t. vanilla extract

Toast pecans in ¹/4 cup butter in 350 degree oven for 20 to 25 minutes. Stir frequently. Sift flour with baking powder and salt. Cream one cup butter. Gradually add sugar to butter, creaming well. Blend in eggs. Add dry ingredients, alternating with milk. Beat well after each addition. Stir in vanilla and toasted pecans. Pour batter into 3 greased and floured 8" or 9" round cake pans. Bake at 350 degrees for 20 to 25 minutes or until a toothpick inserted in the center comes out clean. Cool before frosting.

Frosting:
¹/4 c. butter
1 lb. powdered sugar
1 t. vanilla extract
4 to 6 T. evaporated milk
²/3 c. pecans, toasted and
    chopped

Blend all ingredients, except pecans, with rotary beater. Stir in pecans and frost cake.

Judy Borecky
Escondido, CA

TURTLE SQUARES

Nothing slow about these turtles! Quick to make, and they'll disappear before you know it.

1 c. butter
1 c. plus 1 T. light corn syrup, divided
14-oz. can sweetened condensed milk
2¼ c. brown sugar, packed
¾ t. vanilla extract
¾ c. pecans, toasted and chopped
1 c. milk chocolate chips

Line an 8"x8" pan with foil, including sides, and butter foil. Set pan aside. Melt butter in heavy saucepan. Stir in one cup corn syrup, condensed milk and brown sugar. Stirring mixture constantly, cook until candy thermometer reaches 242 to 248 degrees or firm-ball stage, 20 to 35 minutes. Remove pan from heat; stir in vanilla. Layer toasted pecans in bottom of foil-lined pan, and pour caramel syrup over pecans; cool. Melt chocolate and one tablespoon corn syrup in double boiler over low heat. Cool about 5 minutes; spread over caramel-pecan mixture. Cool until firm, then lift out of pan and cut into squares.

For less stress and more time to really enjoy the holidays, bake early and freeze the goodies.

Sugar Plums, Toffee Delight

SUGAR PLUMS

These are a Christmas tradition at our house...they are yummy!

2 eggs, beaten
1½ c. sugar, divided
1 c. dates, chopped
1 c. coconut
1 c. walnuts, chopped
1 t. vanilla extract

Blend eggs and one cup sugar together. Stir in dates, coconut, walnuts and vanilla. Butter a 2-quart casserole dish and pour in mixture. Bake at 375 degrees for 30 minutes, stirring every 10 minutes. Remove from oven and let cool until mixture can be handled. Roll into walnut-size balls. Roll balls in remaining sugar.

Delores Berg
Selah, WA

TOFFEE DELIGHT

Pack in your favorite old-fashioned tins.

1 c. butter or margarine
1⅓ c. sugar
1 T. light corn syrup
¼ c. water
4-oz. bar milk chocolate
8-oz. pkg. pecans

Melt butter in a heavy saucepan, adding sugar, corn syrup and water. Insert candy thermometer and cook, stirring often, until mixture reaches hard-crack stage, 300 degrees. Pour onto a buttered cookie sheet and cool completely. Melt chocolate bar and spread over top of toffee, then sprinkle with pecans. Chill until hard and break into pieces.

Karen Zartman
Clyde, OH

KRIS KRINGLE CAKE

A special cake for a special time of year.

Cake:
1/2 c. butter or margarine,
    softened
1 1/2 c. brown sugar, packed
3 eggs
1 c. sour cream
1/2 c. milk
2 c. all-purpose flour
2 t. cinnamon
1 1/2 t. baking soda
1 t. baking powder
1/2 t. cloves
1/2 t. nutmeg
1/2 t. salt

Frosting:
6 c. powdered sugar
3/4 c. vegetable shortening
3/4 c. butter or margarine,
    softened
3 T. milk
1 T. vanilla extract
brown and red paste food coloring
red candied cherry, halved
4 lg. marshmallows

Kris Kringle Cake

For cake, cream butter and brown sugar in a large bowl until fluffy. Add eggs, one at a time, beating well after each addition. Add sour cream and milk; stir until well blended. In a medium bowl, sift flour, cinnamon, baking soda, baking powder, cloves, nutmeg and salt. Add dry ingredients to creamed mixture, stirring until well blended. Spoon batter into a greased and floured 12 1/2-inch-wide star-shaped baking pan. Bake at 350 degrees for 35 to 40 minutes or until a toothpick inserted in the center of cake comes out clean. Cool 10 minutes. Remove cake from pan and cool completely on a wire rack.

For frosting, combine powdered sugar, shortening, butter, milk and vanilla in a large bowl; beat until smooth. Spoon 1 1/2 cups frosting

into a pastry bag; cover end of bag with plastic wrap and set aside. Spoon 1/4 cup frosting into small bowl; tint brown. Spoon brown frosting into a pastry bag; cover end of bag with plastic wrap and set aside. Spoon one cup frosting into another small bowl; tint red. Spread remaining white frosting on sides of cake, on top of four tips of cake for hands and feet and on top of cake for face. Spread red frosting on top of cake for hat and suit. Use table knife or small metal spatula dipped in water to smooth frosting. Using white frosting and a basketweave tip with smooth side of tip facing up, pipe stripes on pants and trim on shirt and hat. Using brown frosting and a basketweave tip with smooth side

of tip facing up, pipe belt and trim on top of boots. Using brown frosting and a small round tip, pipe eyes and laces on boots. Using white frosting and a grass tip, pipe beard. Place one cherry half on cake for nose. Cut one marshmallow in half crosswise. Place one marshmallow half on top of hat for pom-pom. Trace mustache and eyebrow patterns, page 157, onto tracing paper; cut out. Use a rolling pin to roll out remaining marshmallows to 1/8-inch thickness. Place patterns on marshmallow pieces and use small sharp knife to cut out 2 mustache pieces and 2 eyebrows; place on cake. Store in an airtight container in refrigerator. Yields about 16 servings.

YUM ★ YUMS
A RICH and GOOEY TREAT!

40 CARAMELS
1/2 c. SWEETENED CONDENSED MILK
1/2 c. MARGARINE
LARGE MARSHMALLOWS
CRISPED RICE CEREAL

★

IN A HEAVY SAUCEPAN, MELT TOGETHER CARAMELS, CONDENSED MILK & MARGARINE OVER LOW HEAT. DIP LARGE MARSHMALLOWS IN MIXTURE ON TOOTHPICK OR BAMBOO SKEWER. ROLL IN CRISPED RICE CEREAL.

Oatmeal Cut-Outs

Always sift your dry ingredients together; baking soda has a tendency to lump when unsifted.

OATMEAL CUT-OUTS
These cookies have been such a long-standing tradition of Christmas for my family and me, I can't imagine not making them.

3/4 c. butter
1/2 c. sugar
1/2 c. brown sugar, packed
1 egg
1 t. vanilla extract
1 2/3 c. all-purpose flour
1 1/2 c. quick-cooking oats
1/2 t. baking soda
1/8 t. salt
powdered sugar

Cream butter, sugar and brown sugar together. Add egg and vanilla and beat well. Blend in dry ingredients, except powdered sugar, and chill overnight. Divide dough and roll out on powdered sugar; cut with your favorite cookie cutters. Bake at 350 degrees for 5 to 8 minutes. Makes approximately 3 dozen cookies, depending on the size of the cookie cutter.

Melissa Gullion
Ottumwa, IA

HOT CRANBERRY PUNCH
The aroma will fill your house with holiday cheer.

3 qts. water
3 c. sugar
1/2 c. red cinnamon candies
1 qt. cranberry juice
1 c. orange juice
1 c. pineapple juice
1/2 c. lemon juice
Garnish: whole cloves

Heat together the water, sugar and red cinnamon candies in a large pan until sugar and red cinnamon candies are fully dissolved. Add remaining ingredients. Sprinkle with whole cloves. Heat and serve. Wonderful!

Denise Green

MINCEMEAT COOKIES

These cookies can become a tradition at your house.

1½ c. all-purpose flour
1½ t. baking soda
¼ c. water
2 eggs
⅓ c. vegetable shortening
¾ c. brown sugar, packed
½ t. cinnamon
¼ t. nutmeg
¼ t. salt
½ c. nuts
½ c. mincemeat

Sift flour and baking soda into a large mixing bowl. Put water, eggs, shortening, brown sugar, spices and salt into blender; cover and process at MIX until smooth. Push CHOP button, remove cover and add nuts and mincemeat, processing only until nuts are chopped. Pour mixture into flour and mix well. Drop by teaspoonfuls onto greased cookie sheet. Bake 8 to 10 minutes. Immediately remove cookies from cookie sheet. Yields about 5 dozen.

Charmaine Hahl
Leesburg, FL

Pumpkin Bars

SOUTHERN PECAN PIE

Perfect for your holiday gathering.

3 eggs
2 T. butter, melted
2 T. all-purpose flour
¼ t. vanilla extract
⅛ t. salt
½ c. sugar
1½ c. light corn syrup
½ c. pecan halves
9-inch pie crust, unbaked

Beat eggs; blend in butter, flour, vanilla, salt, sugar and corn syrup. Sprinkle pecans over pie crust; pour egg mixture over pecans. Bake at 425 degrees for 10 minutes. Reduce heat to 325 degrees and continue baking for 40 minutes or until middle is set.

Susan Bowman
Moline, IL

PUMPKIN BARS

A yummy dessert to make for the holidays.

1 c. all-purpose flour
⅔ c. sugar
1 t. baking powder
1 t. cinnamon
½ t. baking soda
⅛ t. salt
⅛ t. cloves
1 c. canned pumpkin
2 egg whites, slightly beaten
¼ c. oil
¼ c. water

Spray an 11"x7" baking pan with non-stick vegetable spray; set pan aside. In medium mixing bowl, combine flour, sugar, baking powder, cinnamon, baking soda, salt and cloves. Stir in pumpkin, egg whites, oil and water until thoroughly combined. Spread batter into the pan. Bake at 350 degrees for 20 to 25 minutes or until toothpick inserted near center comes out clean. Cool in pan on a wire rack; frost. Cut into 24 bars. Cover and store in refrigerator.

Frosting:
¼ c. cream cheese
1¾ c. powdered sugar, divided
1 t. vanilla extract
¼ t. lemon or orange zest, grated

In medium bowl, beat together cream cheese, one cup powdered sugar, vanilla and grated lemon or orange zest until mixture is light and fluffy. Gradually beat in remaining powdered sugar.

Kathy Grashoff
Fort Wayne, IN

DELICIOUS CUSTARD CAKE PUDDING

Makes 20 servings...perfect for a dessert party!

1 lb. leftover tea bread or
   scones
$1/4$ c. butter
2 tart apples, peeled and sliced
4 oz. dates, chopped, or 4 oz.
   dried cranberries
8 whole eggs plus 4 yolks
$2/3$ c. sugar
$1/2$ t. salt
$1/2$ t. nutmeg
2 T. rum or rum extract
$1^1/2$ qts. milk
$1^1/4$ c. whipping cream
2 10-oz. pkgs. frozen
   raspberries or strawberries
2 T. cornstarch
$1/4$ c. raspberry syrup
Garnish: whipped topping

Crumble bread or scones and spread in bottom of a 13"x9" baking dish. Dot with butter. Arrange sliced apples over the bread and add dates or cranberries. To eggs, add sugar, salt, nutmeg and rum. Beat until well combined. Combine milk and cream; heat to scalding. Carefully add hot milk to egg mixture and stir. Pour over contents in the baking dish. Place pudding dish in a roasting pan; add one inch of hot water. Bake at 375 degrees for 45 minutes or until knife inserted in center comes out dry. When done, remove dish from roasting pan. Thaw and crush raspberries. Put cornstarch in a bowl and add raspberry syrup. Heat in microwave, stirring the cornstarch so there are no lumps. Add to thawed berries; heat until the sauce is slightly thickened. Top individual servings of pudding with whipped topping and about 2 tablespoons of raspberry sauce.

Vintage Tea Room
Escondido, CA

Amaretto Mousse Cheesecake

AMARETTO MOUSSE CHEESECAKE

Scatter sliced almonds on top for a very pretty garnish.

2 c. graham cracker crumbs
$1/2$ c. butter, melted
1 envelope plain gelatin
$1/2$ c. cold water
3 8-oz. pkgs. cream cheese,
   softened
$1^1/4$ c. sugar
5-oz. can evaporated milk
1 t. lemon juice
$1/3$ c. Amaretto liqueur
1 t. vanilla extract
$3/4$ c. whipping cream, whipped
Garnish: sliced almonds

Combine the cracker crumbs with butter. Press into bottom and up sides of a 9" springform pan; chill.

In a small saucepan, sprinkle gelatin over cold water. Let stand one minute. Stir over low heat until completely dissolved, about 3 minutes. Set aside. In a large bowl, beat cream cheese with sugar until fluffy, about 2 minutes. Gradually add the evaporated milk and lemon juice; beat at medium-high speed until mixture is very fluffy, about 2 minutes. Add liqueur or see substitution below. Gradually beat in gelatin mixture and vanilla. Fold in whipped cream. Pour into crust; chill 8 hours or overnight. Garnish with sliced almonds.

To omit Amaretto liqueur, increase water to $3/4$ cup and add $1/2$ teaspoon almond extract in addition to the vanilla.

Jeannine English
Wylie, TX

Chocolate-Covered treats

CHOCOLATE-COVERED CHERRY COOKIES

One of our favorites.

1¹/2 c. all-purpose flour
¹/2 c. cocoa
¹/4 t. salt
¹/4 t. baking powder
¹/4 t. baking soda
¹/2 c. butter, softened
1 c. sugar
1 egg
1¹/2 t. vanilla extract
21-oz. can cherry pie filling,
    reserving 4 t. of filling
    sauce
6-oz. pkg. semi-sweet
    chocolate chips
¹/2 c. sweetened condensed milk

Mix first 5 ingredients together in a small bowl. In a large bowl, beat together butter and sugar until fluffy. Add egg and vanilla; beat well. Gradually add dry ingredients to creamed mixture; beat until well blended. Shape into one-inch balls. Place on ungreased cookie sheet; press down center of dough with thumb. Place a cherry in the center of each cookie. In a small saucepan, combine chocolate chips and sweetened condensed milk; heat until chocolate is melted. Stir in 4 teaspoons of the sauce from pie filling. Spoon about a teaspoon of frosting over each cherry, spreading to cover cherry. Bake in a 350 degree oven about 10 minutes or until cookies begin to look dry. Remove to wire rack to cool. Makes 48 cookies.

Tammy Barnum
Portland, TN

Chocolate-Covered Cherry Cookies, Honey-Nut Christmas Cookies

HONEY-NUT CHRISTMAS COOKIES

These are reminiscent of baklava, but easier to make! Stand back and take the compliments; these are good!

2 c. all-purpose flour
¹/8 t. salt
1 c. butter, chilled
8-oz. pkg. cream cheese
1 c. walnuts
¹/4 c. sugar
6 T. honey
1 t. butter, melted
¹/2 t. cinnamon

Combine flour and salt in a large bowl. Cut up chilled butter and cream cheese and add to flour. With pastry blender or 2 knives, cut in until blended to the consistency of coarse grain. Divide in half; shape dough into 2 balls, wrap and refrigerate for one hour.

Grind nuts with sugar in a food processor, then transfer to a bowl. Stir in honey, butter and cinnamon. Grease 2 cookie sheets. On a well-floured surface, roll one dough ball ¹/8-inch thick and cut into circles using a 2-inch cookie cutter or a floured glass. Place one teaspoon of nut and honey filling on half the circles; top with remaining circles, making a sandwich. Press edges with a fork to seal. Transfer to cookie sheets and bake at 375 degrees for 16 to 18 minutes or until golden. Repeat with remaining dough scraps and filling.

Michele Grippa
Aliquippa, PA

CHRISTMAS CRUNCH

Place in tins and it's ready for gift-giving!

12-oz. pkg. white chocolate
    morsels
1 c. sm. pretzel twists
1 c. apple-cinnamon cereal
1 c. graham cracker cereal
1 c. pecans

Melt morsels over low heat in a saucepan or in the microwave. Combine all other ingredients in a large bowl and pour melted morsels over mixture, stirring well to coat. Line cookie sheets with wax paper; spread mixture on cookie sheets and refrigerate. When completely cool, break into pieces and store in airtight containers.

Mary Lou Traylor
Arlington, TN

ALMOND BRITTLE

Collect Christmas tins and fill 'em with almond brittle for your friends!

1 c. slivered almonds
1/2 c. butter
1/2 c. sugar
1 T. light corn oil

Line a 13"x9" cake pan with foil, butter the foil and set aside. In a non-stick skillet, combine all ingredients over medium heat until they come to a boil, about 5 to 6 minutes, stirring constantly. When mixture turns a golden brown and begins to stick together, pour into pan and work quickly! Spread evenly, cool and break into pieces.

Pat Husek
St. Joseph, MI

Almond Brittle, Pumpkin Cookies with Caramel Frosting, Christmas Crunch

PUMPKIN COOKIES WITH CARAMEL FROSTING

The caramel frosting makes these cookies extra special.

1 c. margarine, softened
1 c. sugar
1 c. canned pumpkin
2 eggs
1 t. vanilla extract
1/8 t. salt
2 c. all-purpose flour
1 t. cinnamon
1 t. baking powder
1 t. baking soda
1 c. chopped walnuts
9-oz. box raisins

Cream margarine, sugar, pumpkin, eggs, vanilla and salt. Sift flour, cinnamon, baking powder and baking soda; add to creamed mixture. Add walnuts and raisins, mixing well. Drop by tablespoonfuls onto an ungreased cookie sheet. Bake at 350 degrees for 15 to 20 minutes. Frost with Caramel Frosting.

Caramel Frosting:
1/4 c. butter
5 T. milk
2/3 c. brown sugar, packed
1 1/4 c. powdered sugar, sifted
1 t. vanilla extract

Combine butter, milk and brown sugar in a medium saucepan. Boil for 2 minutes, stirring constantly. Cool. Stir in powdered sugar and vanilla. Beat until smooth and creamy.

Denise Krasucki

GINGER SPICE BRUNCH!

Early birds and sleepyheads alike will love waking up to a cozy Christmas brunch! Invite your friends over for a merry morning filled with tasty breakfast treats.

GINGER SPICE BREAD

For a special treat, make this delicious bread into gingerbread boys.

1¹/₂ c. plus 1 T. milk, divided
¹/₂ c. plus 2 T. butter or margarine
²/₃ c. molasses
1 T. ginger
1 T. dried orange zest
1 T. cardamom
2 t. cinnamon
1¹/₄ t. salt
1 t. cloves
1 t. nutmeg
2 pkgs. active yeast
1 T. sugar
¹/₃ c. warm water
3 eggs, divided
1¹/₂ c. whole-wheat flour
5 to 6 c. all-purpose flour

Heat 1¹/₂ cups milk and butter over medium heat until butter melts. Remove from heat and stir in molasses, ginger, orange zest, cardamom, cinnamon, salt, cloves and nutmeg. Cool to room temperature.

In a large bowl, dissolve yeast and sugar in water. Add milk mixture and 2 eggs, one at a time, stirring well after each addition. Add whole-wheat flour and enough all-purpose flour to form a soft dough. Turn onto a lightly floured surface and knead 5 minutes or until dough becomes smooth and elastic.

Ginger Spice Bread

Place dough in a large bowl sprayed with vegetable spray, turning once to coat top of dough. Cover and let rise in a warm place, 80 to 85 degrees, one hour or until double in size.

Turn dough onto a lightly floured surface and punch down. Shape dough into 3 round loaves. Transfer to greased baking sheets. Cover and let rise in a warm place 30 minutes or until double in size.

Beat remaining egg and milk; brush over top of loaves. Bake at 350 degrees 20 to 25 minutes or until bread sounds hollow when tapped. Serve warm or transfer to wire rack to cool completely. Makes 3 bread loaves.

For Ginger Spice Boys: Trace pattern, page 157, onto stencil plastic; cut out. Mix dough according to bread recipe. After first rising, turn dough onto a lightly floured surface and punch down. Roll out dough to ³/₄-inch thickness. Use pattern and a sharp knife to cut out shapes. Transfer to

greased baking sheets. Decorate each gingerbread boy with red licorice for mouth and raisins for eyes. Cover and let rise in a warm place 30 minutes or until double in size. Follow bread recipe to bake. Makes about 7 gingerbread boys.

TOMATO COCKTAIL

A great appetizer to serve while you're putting the finishing touches on brunch.

46-oz. can tomato juice
juice of ¹/₂ a lemon
1 t. sweet onion, grated
1 t. Worcestershire sauce
¹/₈ t. hot pepper sauce
Garnish: celery sticks

Combine all ingredients together; chill. Serves 6.

COTTAGE POTATOES

Every time I serve these potatoes someone requests the recipe!

8 to 10 potatoes, boiled until
    tender
8 oz. pasteurized process
    cheese spread, cubed
1 green pepper, diced
2-oz. jar pimentos, diced and
    drained
1 onion, diced
¹/₂ c. margarine, melted
¹/₂ c. milk
1 bread slice, torn
2 T. fresh parsley, chopped
salt and pepper

Peel potatoes and slice into chunks; mix with cheese, green pepper, pimento and onion. Combine remaining ingredients and add to potato mixture. Place in a greased 2¹/₂-quart casserole dish and bake at 350 degrees for 45 to 50 minutes.

Delores Hollenbeck
Omaha, NE

Cottage Potatoes, Christmas Casserole, Tomato Cocktail

CHRISTMAS CASSEROLE

A Christmas Day favorite; make it the day before and just pop it in the oven!

5¹/₂-oz. pkg. seasoned croutons
1 lb. bulk sausage, cooked,
    crumbled and drained
4 eggs
2 c. milk
16-oz. pkg. frozen Italian
    vegetables, thawed
10³/₄-oz. can cream of
    mushroom soup
1 c. Cheddar cheese, shredded
1 c. Monterey Jack cheese,
    shredded

Line the bottom of a 13"x9" baking pan with the croutons. Sprinkle cooked sausage over the croutons. Beat eggs and milk until thoroughly mixed and add remaining ingredients, stirring well. Pour egg mixture over the sausage. Bake at 350 degrees for one hour. Casserole may be prepared ahead and refrigerated before baking. Serves 8.

Flour your cookie cutters to help keep them from sticking! Since cookie cutters can rust, dry them completely, then use a hair dryer, set at cool, to remove all water. You can even flour them again and store in a plastic bag.

JEAN'S COFFEE CAKE

This coffee cake recipe is my favorite because it reminds me of my sister. Now that she's no longer with us, I continue the tradition of making this coffee cake each Christmas and it always sparks fond memories of her.

Coffee Cake:
1/2 c. butter, softened
1 c. sugar
3 eggs, lightly beaten
1 t. baking powder
1 t. baking soda
2 c. all-purpose flour
1 c. sour cream
2 c. fresh raspberries or frozen, thawed and drained

Topping:
1 c. brown sugar, packed
1/4 c. butter, softened
1/4 c. all-purpose flour

For coffee cake, cream butter and sugar; add eggs, baking powder and baking soda. Alternately add flour and sour cream to mixture and fold in raspberries. Pour into a well-buttered Bundt® pan. For topping, combine brown sugar and butter, mixing well. Add flour; mixture will be lumpy. Spread on coffee cake batter; bake at 350 degrees for 35 to 45 minutes or until a toothpick inserted in center comes out clean.

Deborah Brown
Pasadena, CA

Jean's Coffee Cake

APRICOT-PECAN BREAD

A delicious addition to Christmas brunch.

1/4 c. butter or margarine, softened
1 1/4 c. sugar
1 egg, beaten
2 c. all-purpose flour, sifted
1/2 t. baking powder
1/2 t. baking soda
1/2 t. salt
1 T. coriander
1 c. canned apricots, mashed and drained
2 T. sour cream
1/2 t. almond extract
1/2 c. pecans, chopped
1/2 c. maraschino cherries, halved

Grease and flour loaf pan. Beat butter and sugar in large bowl and stir in egg. Mix sifted flour, baking powder, baking soda, salt and coriander on a piece of wax paper. Stir into sugar mixture. Fold in apricots, sour cream and almond extract. Stir in pecans and cherries. Turn into the prepared pan. Bake at 350 degrees for 50 minutes. Cool for 5 minutes. Remove from pan and cool completely. Wrap in foil or plastic wrap. Refrigerate. Allow flavors to blend for 24 hours before serving.

Marion Pfeifer
Smyrna, DE

Freshly-baked coffee cake makes a welcome gift! Tuck it in a round basket lined with cheery red fabric. Trim the edge of the basket with greenery, cinnamon sticks, bay leaves and sprigs of berries. Tie your gift card to the handle with several strands of raffia.

"All happiness depends on a leisurely breakfast."

— John Gunther

OLD-FASHIONED DOUGHNUTS

My aunt used to make these doughnuts when I was growing up in the 1950's. She would make them on Sunday evenings and invite all my family to her big old farmhouse to share them for supper. The grownups would drink coffee and talk while she made doughnuts, then everyone would dip them in glaze or sugar and eat too many!

2 pkgs. active yeast
1 T. sugar
1 c. lukewarm water
1 c. milk
6 T. vegetable shortening
1/2 c. sugar
1 t. salt
7 c. all-purpose flour, sifted and
    divided
3 eggs, beaten

Dissolve yeast and sugar in water. Scald milk; add shortening, sugar and salt. Cool to lukewarm. Add 2 cups of flour to make a batter.

Add yeast and eggs and beat well. Add remaining flour to make a soft dough. Knead lightly and place in a greased bowl, turning once. Cover and let rise in a warm place until double in size. Roll out to 1/2-inch thickness. Cut into doughnuts; let rise again until double. Fry in hot oil until brown. Dip in powdered sugar glaze or sugar.

Cheryl Fancher
Okawville, IL

STRAWBERRY BUTTER

Good on French toast or bagels.

1/2 lb. butter, softened
10-oz. pkg. frozen strawberries,
    thawed and drained
1/2 c. powdered sugar

Combine all ingredients with a mixer or in a food processor until smooth and creamy. Serve at room temperature.

Jo Ann

FRENCH TOAST WAFFLES

If you need to reheat, just pop in the toaster!

4 eggs
1/2 c. milk
2 T. butter, melted
1 T. sugar
1/2 t. salt
8 to 10 bread slices

Preheat waffle iron. Spray with a light coating of vegetable spray. In a shallow bowl, combine eggs, milk, melted butter, sugar and salt. Dip bread slices, one at a time, in egg mixture. Bake in waffle iron 2 to 3 minutes or until brown. Top with Strawberry Butter.

Jo Ann

Top your coffee with spicy whipped cream. Whip 1/2 cup whipping cream with 2 tablespoons powdered sugar and 1/4 teaspoon ground cinnamon, then add a dash of nutmeg!

Fill a bowl with whole nutmegs and a nutmeg grater. Guests will love fresh nutmeg in their coffee!

Holly's Hot Mocha, Old-Fashioned Doughnuts

HOLLY'S HOT MOCHA*

A SERIOUSLY YUMMY BLEND OF COCOA & COFFEE

INGREDIENTS:

- 1-1/4 t. CHOCOLATE SYRUP
- 3/4 c. STRONG COFFEE
- 2 T. HOT MILK
- DOLLOP OF WHIPPED CREAM
- CHOCOLATE SHAVINGS

PLACE CHOCOLATE SYRUP, COFFEE & HOT MILK IN A MUG. TOP WITH DOLLOP OF WHIPPED CREAM & CHOCOLATE SHAVINGS.

* NOTE: BEST CONSUMED IN FRONT OF BLAZING FIRE, WRAPPED IN CASHMERE THROW & SHARED WITH MOVIE-STAR TYPE MALE BLESSED WITH RIPPLING BICEPS, CHIN CLEFT & ADORING PERSONALITY. JUST A SUGGESTION, COUNTRY FRIEND-TO-COUNTRY FRIEND

In the Company of Friends!

Shrimp Mousse, Roquefort Cut-Out Crackers

What better way to spend Christmas than in the company of friends! This year, host an open house they'll never forget. Invite friends, family…everyone you know! Get your guests in the holiday spirit by building a cozy fire, playing Christmas tunes and filling your house with fresh greenery, glowing candles and cinnamon pine cones. Have everyone bring a homemade ornament to exchange, or do something traditional like stringing popcorn and singing carols. But whatever you do, don't forget to fill your table with an abundance of yummy treats to munch on…like our luscious lasagna rolls, spicy salsa and scrumptious cream cheese truffles. And most importantly, just have fun, be merry and enjoy the warmth of friendship and family!

SHRIMP MOUSSE

A creamy spread that's yummy on crackers.

8-oz. pkg. cream cheese
1 envelope plain gelatin
1/4 c. warm water
1 c. mayonnaise
10 3/4-oz. can cream of
    mushroom soup
1/2 c. celery, diced
1/2 c. onion, finely chopped
2 c. frozen or fresh small salad
    shrimp, chopped
Garnish: lemon slices and fresh
    parsley

Melt cream cheese over low heat using a double boiler. Dissolve gelatin in 1/4 cup warm water. Add to softened cream cheese and stir until smooth. Add other ingredients and pour into an oiled fish-shaped mold. Refrigerate until solid. Unmold onto lemon slices on serving plate; garnish with fresh parsley. Makes 5 cups.

Barbara Truax
St. Louis, MO

ROQUEFORT CUT-OUT CRACKERS

Delicate cheese wafers with a touch of hot pepper!

1 c. unbleached flour
7 T. Roquefort cheese crumbles
1 egg yolk
4 t. whipping cream
7 T. butter, softened
1/8 t. salt
cayenne pepper to taste
1/2 t. dried parsley flakes

Mix all ingredients together and roll into a dough. Let rest for half an hour, then roll dough out to about 1/8-inch thickness. Use a round cookie cutter to cut out crackers. Bake on an ungreased cookie sheet at 400 degrees for 7 to 9 minutes. Cool on cookie sheet.

Lasagna Rolls

LASAGNA ROLLS

When I was little, I remember standing on a chair next to my mom by the stove. I watched her roll these little bundles of noodles, meat and cheese and I would beg her to let me roll up a few. She always let me try some, and even though they were nothing compared to hers, she made me feel like they were perfect.

1 lb. mild or sage bulk sausage,
    cooked, crumbled and
    drained
8-oz. plus 3-oz. pkgs. cream
    cheese
1 green onion bunch, chopped
1 green pepper, diced
26-oz. jar spaghetti sauce
16 lasagna noodles, uncooked
1 1/2 c. mozzarella cheese,
    shredded

Combine sausage and cream cheese in the skillet where sausage was browned. Cook over low heat until cream cheese melts. Stir in onion and green pepper; remove from heat. Spread half the spaghetti sauce in the bottom of a 13"x9" baking dish; set aside. Cook lasagna noodles according to package directions; remove from heat and leave in water. Lay one noodle flat on a cutting board and spoon one to 2 tablespoons of sausage mixture at one end of the noodle. Slowly roll the noodle and place in baking dish. Repeat with remaining noodles. Pour reserved sauce over top of rolls; top with mozzarella. Bake at 350 degrees for 15 to 20 minutes or until cheese has melted.

Kelli Keeton
Delaware, OH

The art of dining well is no slight art, the pleasure not a slight pleasure.
– MONTAIGNE

Gather your friends together and serve

HERB & GARLIC Dip

(But save some for yourself!)

Fresh Herb & Garlic Dip, Jeff's Dried Beef Dip

FRESH HERB & GARLIC DIP

Serve with fresh vegetables or chips.

1 c. low-fat sour cream
1 c. low-fat mayonnaise
2 T. fresh parsley, chopped
2 T. fresh chives, chopped
1 T. fresh thyme, chopped
1 T. fresh rosemary, chopped
2 T. garlic chives, chopped
1 garlic clove, pressed

Mix sour cream, mayonnaise, herbs and garlic in a glass bowl. Cover and refrigerate overnight. Makes 2 cups.

DiAnn Voegele
Mascoutah, IL

F*a-la-la-la-la-la-la-la-la…At your neighborhood Christmas party, invite the local high school choir to come caroling. This will be a delightful surprise for all the guests!*

JEFF'S DRIED BEEF DIP

Warm slices of French bread or wheat crackers are all you'll need to serve with this; it's wonderful!

1/2 c. pecans, chopped
2 T. butter
1/2 t. salt
8-oz. plus 3-oz. pkgs. cream cheese, softened
1 onion, finely chopped
2 1/2-oz. pkg. dried beef, chopped
1/4 c. green pepper, chopped
2 T. milk
1 c. sour cream
pepper to taste

Combine pecans, butter and salt; spread on a cookie sheet. Place in oven under broiler and lightly toast for 3 to 5 minutes. Remove from oven and set aside. Mix next 5 ingredients; fold in sour cream, half the pecan mixture and pepper. Place in a 13"x9" baking dish and sprinkle remaining pecan mixture over top. Bake at 350 degrees for 20 minutes. Makes about 3 cups.

Sherry Sellers
Sunbury, OH

HOT CRAB DIP

Try a basket of baked pita chips with this.

1/2 lb. fresh crab, shelled
2 8-oz. pkgs. cream cheese
1 onion, grated
1 T. horseradish sauce
2 T. whipping cream
1 t. salt
1/2 t. garlic powder
1/2 t. white pepper
2 drops hot pepper sauce

Mix all ingredients together. Place in a fondue pot or heat in a 350 degree oven for 20 minutes or until heated thoroughly.

Lesli Jo Krieger
Deer Park, WA

WINE-MARINATED BEEF BRISKET

Serve with an assortment of breads and flavored mustards for sandwiches.

1 c. dry red wine
1 celery stalk, thinly sliced
1 onion, grated
2 T. soy sauce
2 garlic cloves, minced
3 to 3½ lbs. brisket, trimmed
1 onion, thinly sliced

Mix together the first 5 ingredients and put in a glass baking dish. Add the brisket and turn over in the marinade so it's completely coated. Cover meat and allow to marinate for several hours in the refrigerator, turning occasionally. If your brisket is still frozen, you can let it thaw while it sits in the marinade. Transfer brisket to a large iron skillet and arrange the sliced onion around it. Pour half the marinade over the meat, reserving the rest. Cover the pan with aluminum foil or a tightly-fitting lid and roast at 325 degrees, basting occasionally, for about 3 hours or until tender. If the meat seems to be drying out, boil reserved marinade and add to meat while it cooks. Remove from the oven and let cool a bit before you slice thinly and transfer the meat to a serving dish. Pour any pan juices over the slices. Serves about 8 as a main dish or serve cold with sandwich buns and horseradish.

Dress your holiday table for winter…use whimsical mittens to hold your napkins and silverware and lay woolen scarves across the table to serve as place mats. Enamelware plates and cups add rustic charm.

Hooray for Santa Claus! He's a definite country friend, for sure.

Wine-Marinated Beef Brisket

WOW! Holiday Appetizers

HERBED POPCORN

This quick snack will feed a crowd.

1/2 t. dried marjoram
1/2 t. dried basil
1/2 t. garlic salt
1/2 c. butter, melted
20 c. popped corn

Mix herbs and garlic salt and add to melted butter. Pour over popcorn.

Judy Carter

COCKTAIL WALNUTS

Just the right amount of seasoning makes these nuts special.

3 T. vegetable oil
8 oz. walnuts
2 t. celery salt
1/4 t. garlic powder
1/4 t. cayenne pepper

In a skillet, heat the oil, stir in the walnuts and sauté. Stir constantly until crisp. Remove nuts with a slotted spoon. Mix together salt, garlic powder and pepper. Toss nuts in this mixture.

Judy Carter

Hot Buttered Cider, Herbed Popcorn, Hot Party Nuts

HOT BUTTERED CIDER

A spicy aroma that fills the air on a cool winter evening.

2 qts. apple cider
2 1/2 c. rum, optional
juice of 2 oranges
juice of 2 lemons
15 whole cloves
6 cinnamon sticks
1 T. honey
1 T. allspice
1 t. cinnamon
3 T. butter

Simmer all ingredients, except butter, in a pot over medium heat for about 30 minutes. Strain if you like; stir in butter and serve hot.

HOT PARTY NUTS

These nuts have been a family favorite ever since my sister served them at her house-warming. This recipe is delicious made with peanuts; even better with cashews!

3/4 lb. nuts
1 egg white, beaten
2 t. kosher salt
1 t. sugar
1 t. red pepper flakes
1/2 t. cumin
1/2 t. oregano
1/4 t. cayenne pepper

Toss nuts in egg white; sprinkle seasonings over nuts. Bake at 300 degrees for 25 minutes.

Richard Welsh
Gooseberry Patch

SALSA

A quick and easy salsa, but not short on taste!

28-oz. can whole tomatoes, drained and chopped
1 onion, chopped
3 jalapeño peppers, chopped
1 oz. white vinegar
1 oz. lime juice
1 T. garlic salt
1 T. vegetable oil
1 T. fresh cilantro, chopped

Combine all ingredients. Chill and serve with your favorite taco chips.

Sheryl Desrocheis

An interesting way to serve cold drinks at a party is to line your favorite basket with plastic and fill with crushed ice. This will keep miniature bottles of wine, soft drinks or bottled water cold and at people's fingertips.

SPICY CHEESE BALL

This cheese ball can be made ahead.

1½ lbs. sharp Cheddar cheese
4 3-oz. pkgs. cream cheese, softened
8 garlic cloves, minced
4 fresh pimento peppers, chopped
2 to 3 T. chili powder
salt and pepper
1 lb. toasted peanuts, crushed and divided
mayonnaise
chili powder

Shred Cheddar cheese. Mix cream cheese, Cheddar cheese, garlic and pimento peppers. Add 2 to 3 tablespoons chili powder. Salt and pepper to taste. Add ¾ of crushed peanuts. Mix with enough mayonnaise to mold. Use your hands to shape into a ball. Roll in remainder of crushed peanuts. Dust with chili powder. Refrigerate.

PIMENTO DEVILED EGGS

Festive, colorful and tasty!

12 eggs, hard-boiled and peeled
2-oz. jar pimentos, chopped and drained
¼ c. mayonnaise
1½ t. Dijon mustard
½ t. cayenne pepper
¼ t. salt
Garnish: fresh parsley and minced red pepper

Slice each egg lengthwise in half and remove yolk. Mash yolks with a fork. Stir in pimentos, mayonnaise, mustard, cayenne pepper and salt. Spoon yolk mixture into egg-white halves. For a more festive look, pipe the yolks into the whites with a star tip. Refrigerate, covered, until ready to serve. Garnish with fresh parsley and a colorful sprinkling of red pepper. Makes 24.

Pimento Deviled Eggs

mmmmmm Mommy's Hot Salsa circa 1967

STOP DREAMING and START EATING !!

Feeling stressed? Instead of full-course, sit-down dinners, plan informal get-togethers. Buffets are easy to plan; let everyone bring a favorite dish.

107

Holly's Holiday Stress-Buster:

Laugh a lot.

Wear a Santa hat or silly antlers. Give joke gifts. Tell bad knock-knock jokes.

ORANGE SPICE CAKE

A perfect holiday cake!

1/2 c. vegetable shortening
1 c. sugar
2 eggs
2 c. all-purpose flour
1 t. baking soda
1 t. cinnamon
1/2 t. salt
1/2 t. cloves
1/2 t. allspice
2/3 c. milk
1 T. white vinegar
1/3 c. orange juice
1/2 c. walnuts and raisins

Cream shortening; add sugar and eggs. Add dry ingredients. Blend milk and vinegar, stirring alternately into batter with orange juice; beat well. Add walnuts and raisins. Pour into a tube pan; bake at 350 degrees for 45 minutes. Yield: 10 to 12 servings.

Leona Keeley

Easy Cream Cheese Truffles

EASY CREAM CHEESE TRUFFLES

It's fun rolling these in the different coatings.

8-oz. pkg. cream cheese,
   softened
4 1/4 c. powdered sugar, divided
5 oz. unsweetened chocolate,
   melted and cooled
1/4 c. cocoa
1/4 c. almonds, toasted and
   finely chopped
1/4 c. coconut flakes, toasted

Beat cream cheese until fluffy. Slowly add 4 cups powdered sugar. Beat until smooth. Add melted chocolate and beat until blended. Chill for approximately one hour. Shape chilled mixture into one-inch balls. Roll some in 1/4 cup powdered sugar, some in cocoa, some in nuts and some in coconut. Store in an airtight container in the refrigerator for 2 weeks. Makes 6 1/2 dozen truffles.

Jeannine English
Wylie, TX

108

FROSTY'S FAVORITE SNOWBALL COOKIES

2 c. sifted powdered sugar
6 c. crispy rice cereal
1 c. raisins
1 c. chopped pecans
4 c. mini marshmallows
1/4 c. melted butter or margarine
1 t. vanilla extract
1/2 t. almond extract

Put powdered sugar in a big bowl. In another bowl, mix cereal, raisins & pecans.

In a saucepan, combine butter & marshmallows. Stirring constantly, cook over medium heat 'til smooth. Remove from heat & stir in extracts. Pour marshmallow mixture over cereal mixture ~ stir well 'til coated.

Grease hands ~ shape mixture into 1 1/2 - 2" balls and roll in sugar. Store in airtight container.

FESTIVE EGGNOG PUNCH
A good punch for the holidays.

1 qt. eggnog, chilled
2 pts. peppermint ice cream, softened
1 c. ginger ale, chilled

Blend ingredients together. Pour into a punch bowl. Hang small candy canes around bowl.

Caren Schulze
Arlington Heights, IL

DEEP DISH BROWNIES
They almost taste like fudge!

1 c. plus 2 T. butter, melted
2 1/4 c. sugar
2 t. vanilla extract
4 eggs
1 c. plus 2 T. all-purpose flour
3/4 c. cocoa
3/4 t. baking powder
3/4 t. salt
1 3/4 c. semi-sweet chocolate chips

Grease a 13"x9" pan. In a medium mixing bowl, blend butter, sugar and vanilla. Add eggs and beat well with a spoon. In a separate bowl, combine flour, cocoa, baking powder and salt. Gradually add to egg mixture. Beat well until blended. Stir in chocolate chips and spread in prepared pan. Bake at 350 degrees for 40 to 45 minutes or until brownies begin to pull away from sides of pan. Cool completely and cut into 2-inch squares. Makes 24 brownies.

Ann Fehr
Collegeville, PA

GRAMMA'S SNAPPIEST EVER GINGER SNAP COOKIES
The smell of these baking will bring back memories.

3/4 c. vegetable shortening
1 1/2 c. sugar, divided
1/4 c. molasses
1 egg
2 c. all-purpose flour, sifted
2 t. baking soda
1 t. ginger
1 t. cloves
1 t. cinnamon

Cream shortening. Add one cup sugar, molasses and egg. Beat well and add sifted dry ingredients. Beat until smooth. Mixture will be very stiff. Shape a teaspoonful of mixture into a ball; then roll ball in remaining sugar. Bake on a greased cookie sheet at 350 degrees for 10 to 12 minutes.

Karen Roberts

Festive Eggnog Punch, Gramma's Snappiest Ever Ginger Snap Cookies, Deep Dish Brownies

Farmhouse FEAST

Set the table and ring the dinner bell…gather the whole family for an old-fashioned Christmas-Day feast.

APPLE & PEAR-SHAPED CHEESE BALLS

An elegant addition to any holiday party!

¹⁄₄ lb. blue cheese, crumbled
8 oz. sharp Cheddar cheese, finely shredded
2 3-oz. pkgs. cream cheese, softened
1 t. Worcestershire sauce
paprika
2 T. Parmesan cheese, grated
2 drops yellow food coloring
cinnamon stick
lemon leaves

Mix blue cheese, Cheddar cheese, cream cheese and Worcestershire sauce in a medium bowl with a fork until blended. Cover and chill at least 8 hours. Divide cheese mixture in half. Shape one half into a ball and place on wax paper. Sprinkle another piece of wax paper with paprika; roll cheese ball in paprika until thoroughly coated. Mold into an apple shape. Shape the remaining cheese mixture into a ball. Combine Parmesan cheese and food coloring in a covered container or large plastic resealable bag and add cheese ball. Roll cheese ball in Parmesan cheese mixture until thoroughly coated. Mold into a pear shape. Make a small depression in the top of each cheese ball for stem ends; insert piece of cinnamon stick into depressions. Insert leaves into tops of cheese balls. Each cheese ball serves 12.

Martha Terrell
Dillwyn, VA

Apple & Pear-Shaped Cheese Balls, Sparkling Punch

SPARKLING PUNCH
A tangy, bubbly treat!

3 T. sugar
12 whole allspice
3 short cinnamon sticks
8 c. cranberry juice, divided
3 bottles pink champagne or
    ginger ale

In a saucepan over high heat, combine sugar, allspice, cinnamon and 2 cups cranberry juice. Reduce heat to low; cover and simmer 10 minutes. Cool and refrigerate. In pitcher or punch bowl, strain cranberry mixture; discard spices. Add remaining cranberry juice and champagne. Serve at once. Yields 16 cups.

Kathy Bolyea
Naples, FL

BACON-CHEDDAR PUFFS
An easy appetizer with a great combination of flavors! These can be made ahead of time and reheated before you're ready to serve them.

1/2 c. milk
2 T. margarine
1/2 c. all-purpose flour
2 eggs
1/2 c. Cheddar cheese, shredded
4 bacon slices, crisply cooked
    and crumbled
1/4 c. green onion, chopped
1/4 t. garlic salt
1/4 t. pepper

Bring milk and margarine to a boil over medium heat. Add flour all at once, stirring until mixture forms a ball. Remove from heat and add eggs one at a time; blend until smooth. Add Cheddar cheese, bacon, green onion, garlic salt and pepper; mix well. Drop by teaspoonfuls onto greased cookie sheet. Bake at 350 degrees for 5 to 8 minutes. Makes 3 dozen.

Betty McKay
Harmony, MN

Creamy Butternut Soup

CREAMY BUTTERNUT SOUP
Warm and comforting.

5 lbs. butternut squash, peeled
    and chopped
1 1/2 lbs. Red Delicious apples,
    peeled and quartered
1-inch cinnamon stick
2 qts. chicken stock
1 1/2 c. butter
1/3 c. maple syrup
1/2 t. nutmeg
1 pt. light cream

Steam squash, apples and cinnamon stick together until squash is tender. Remove cinnamon stick and place remaining mixture through a food mill or food processor. Pour into a large saucepan. Stir in chicken stock, butter, syrup and nutmeg; simmer 15 minutes. In a small saucepan, heat cream until hot, but not boiling. Add to soup mixture and stir well. Serves 8.

Jo Ann

RED PEPPER SOUP

Spicy, but not too hot, it's a nice change from traditional rice soups.

6 sweet red peppers, chopped
2 carrots, chopped
2 onions, chopped
1 celery stalk, chopped
4 garlic cloves, minced
1 T. olive oil
2 32-oz. cans chicken broth
1/2 c. long grain rice, uncooked
2 t. dried thyme
1 1/2 t. salt
1/4 t. pepper
1/8 to 1/4 t. cayenne pepper
1/8 to 1/4 t. crushed red pepper
    flakes

In a large Dutch oven, sauté red peppers, carrots, onions, celery and garlic in olive oil until tender. Stir in broth, rice, thyme, salt, pepper and cayenne pepper; bring to a boil. Reduce heat; cover and simmer for 20 to 25 minutes or until vegetables and rice are tender. Cool for 30 minutes. Purée in small batches, return to pan and add red pepper flakes. Heat through. Yields 12 cups.

Donna Nowicki
Center City, MN

Red Pepper Soup, Savory Herb Biscuits, Christmas Crunch Salad

SALAD

NO BIG DEAL.

JUST A LITTLE DISH I TOSSED TOGETHER.

CHRISTMAS CRUNCH SALAD

This salad is particularly pretty when served in a clear glass bowl.

Dressing:
1 c. mayonnaise
1 T. vinegar
1/8 t. salt
1/8 t. pepper
1/2 c. sour cream
2 T. sugar

Salad:
2 broccoli bunches, broken
    in small pieces
1 cauliflower head, broken in
    small pieces
1 red onion, chopped
2 c. cherry tomatoes, cut in
    half

Combine dressing ingredients; mix well. Toss with vegetables. Serve well chilled. Can be made a day ahead. Serves 6.

Aundra Zack
Meadville, PA

SAVORY HERB BISCUITS

Delicious and very easy!

2 c. biscuit baking mix
1/2 c. Cheddar cheese, shredded
2/3 c. milk
1/2 t. dried basil leaves
1/2 t. garlic powder
1/4 c. butter or margarine,
    melted

Combine biscuit mix, cheese and milk until a soft dough forms. Beat vigorously for 30 seconds. Roll out dough to 1/2-inch thickness and cut with a star-shaped cookie cutter or drop by heaping tablespoonfuls onto an ungreased cookie sheet. Bake at 450 degrees for 10 to 12 minutes or until golden brown. Combine basil and garlic powder with melted butter and brush over hot biscuits after removing from oven. Makes 12 biscuits.

Jackie Hoover
Newark, OH

PRETZEL SALAD

My mother serves Pretzel Salad on special occasions such as birthdays and Christmas. Everyone always asks for a second helping!

Crust:
2 c. pretzels, crushed
3/4 c. butter, melted
3 T. sugar

Mix crust ingredients together and spread in a 13"x9" baking pan. Bake at 350 degrees for 10 minutes. Cool.

Filling:
8-oz. pkg. cream cheese, softened
1 c. sugar
8 oz. whipped topping, thawed

Combine filling ingredients and spread evenly over crust.

Topping:
2 3-oz. pkgs. strawberry gelatin
2 c. boiling water
2 10-oz. pkgs. frozen strawberries, thawed

Dissolve gelatin in boiling water. Drain juice from strawberries and mix with gelatin mixture. Add strawberries and allow to firm slightly before spreading over filling.

Stephanie Ortner
Whittier, CA

MANDARIN ORANGE SALAD

Quick and easy to prepare; it's best topped with fresh dressing like Raspberry Vinaigrette.

Raspberry Vinaigrette:
1 1/3 c. raspberry vinegar
1 1/3 c. seedless raspberry jam
1 1/2 T. dried coriander
2 t. salt
1 t. pepper
3 c. olive oil

Salad:
3 to 4 c. green or red loose leaf lettuce, torn into bite-size pieces
15-oz. can mandarin oranges, drained
1/2 c. walnut pieces, toasted
1/2 red onion, sliced

For raspberry vinaigrette, combine first 5 ingredients in an electric blender. Turn blender on high, gradually adding oil. Chill. Toss all salad ingredients together. Toss with dressing and serve.

Teena Kellam
Diboll, TX

Mandarin Orange Salad

APPLE ORCHARD GREEN BEANS

Apples add a good flavor to these beans.

2 c. fresh or frozen green beans,
    cut into 2-inch pieces
1 c. carrots, thinly sliced
2 green onions, chopped
1/2 c. water

1 t. sugar
1/4 t. dried thyme, crushed
1/3 c. apple juice
1 t. cornstarch
1/2 c. Red Delicious apple,
    chopped

Combine green beans, carrots, onions, water, sugar and thyme in a large saucepan. Bring to a boil, then reduce heat to low. Cover and simmer until vegetables are crisp-tender. Pour apple juice into a small mixing bowl; blend in cornstarch, stirring until dissolved. Stir into vegetables; stir in apple. Continue to simmer for 2 minutes or until sauce has thickened. Serves 6.

JoAnn

Savory Herb Biscuits, Make-Ahead Dinner Rolls, New England Corn Pudding

Stuffed Tenderloin

STUFFED BEEF TENDERLOIN

Stuffed with spinach and cheese, this roast is so tender you can cut it with a fork!

10-oz. pkg. frozen chopped
    spinach, thawed and drained
1/4 c. dried currants
3 oz. Muenster cheese, grated
1 egg
2 t. balsamic vinegar
1 garlic clove, minced
1/2 t. salt
1/2 t. pepper
6-lb. beef tenderloin, butterflied
1/3 c. beef broth

Place spinach in a large mixing bowl and add currants, cheese, egg, vinegar, garlic, salt and pepper; blend well. Open and flatten tenderloin and spoon spinach mixture down the center of the meat. Bring long sides of meat together; cover filling and tie with butcher's twine at one-inch intervals. Place roast in a shallow baking dish and cover with beef broth. Bake uncovered for 10 minutes at 425 degrees; reduce heat to 350 degrees and bake an additional 25 minutes for rare or 35 minutes for medium-rare. Let tenderloin sit for 15 minutes before carving.

Donna Dye
London, OH

HORSERADISH SAUCE

Low-fat and tasty!

3 T. horseradish, grated
1 c. low-fat mayonnaise
1 t. Dijon mustard

Combine ingredients and refrigerate until needed. Makes about one cup.

Jo Baker
Litchfield, IL

NEW ENGLAND CORN PUDDING

A wonderful, old-fashioned recipe. Make two…one is just never enough!

1/2 c. all-purpose flour
1/2 c. sugar
1 t. salt
1/4 c. sweet, unsalted butter,
    melted
2 c. whole kernel corn, drained
4 eggs
1 qt. whole milk

Stir the flour, sugar, salt and melted butter into the corn. Beat the eggs slightly and combine with the milk. Combine the milk and corn mixtures and pour into a 13"x9" baking dish that has been sprayed with non-stick vegetable spray. Place baking dish in a roasting pan. Add hot water to roasting pan to come halfway up sides of baking dish. Bake in a 350 degree oven for about one hour or until set in center.

The Governor's Inn
Ludlow, VT

Mary Elizabeth's Best SMASHED TATERS

Not technically a dessert but they qualify as a pure pleasure, that's for sure!

3 lbs. peeled & quartered potatoes
1 c. grated parmesan cheese
1/2 c. butter
3 green onions, sliced
1 clove garlic, minced
1/2 c. whipping cream
....

Cook taters in a pan of boiling water 'til very tender—about 25 minutes. Drain; return to pan. Beat with electric mixer.

In another bowl, combine cheese, butter, onions & garlic. Beat with mixer 'til mixture is almost smooth.

Add cheese mixture to potatoes & cream. Beat with electric mixer until very creamy. Season with salt & pepper to taste.

mmmmarvelous!

APRICOT HOLIDAY HAM

A favorite for the buffet table.

5-lb. boneless ham, fully cooked
whole cloves
18-oz. jar apricot preserves
2 t. cornstarch
1 t. orange zest, finely shredded
½ c. orange or pineapple juice
⅛ t. cinnamon
20-oz. can pineapple slices,
   drained

Place ham on a rack in a shallow baking pan. Score top of ham in a diamond pattern, making cuts about ¼-inch deep. Stud with whole cloves. Insert a meat thermometer into center of ham. Bake at 325 degrees about 2 hours or until thermometer registers 140 degrees. Combine apricot preserves and cornstarch in a small saucepan. Stir in orange zest, orange or pineapple juice and cinnamon. Cook and stir until thickened and bubbly. Top ham with pineapple slices. Spoon some of the preserves mixture over the ham 2 or 3 times during the last 30 minutes of baking. Before serving, discard cloves and slice ham thinly. Serve with remaining sauce and pineapple slices. Serves 20.

Tami Bowman
Gooseberry Patch

Make-Ahead Dinner Rolls, Mom's Red Cabbage, Apricot Holiday Ham

MAKE-AHEAD DINNER ROLLS

A county fair blue ribbon winner...so easy for busy days!

1 pkg. active yeast
½ c. sugar
1 c. warm milk
2 eggs, beaten
½ c. butter, melted
1 t. salt
4 c. all-purpose flour

Mix together first 3 ingredients and let stand for 30 minutes. Add next 3 ingredients, then mix in flour, 2 cups at a time. Cover and chill until ready to bake. Divide the dough in half, rolling each half into a 9-inch circle. Cut each circle into 12 equal pie-shaped wedges, a pizza cutter works great, and roll up beginning at the wide end. Place on a well-greased cookie sheet and let rise until double in size. Bake at 375 degrees for 12 to 15 minutes.

Clara Hilton
Marengo, OH

Leave a loaf of bread on the table after Christmas Eve supper and you will have a full supply until the next Christmas.

— Early American folklore

MOM'S RED CABBAGE

This is my favorite recipe because of its great aroma while cooking.

10 bacon slices, diced
1 onion, diced
1 red cabbage head, shredded
1 bay leaf
1/2 c. sugar
1/3 c. vinegar
1 t. chicken bouillon
1 c. applesauce
1 c. jellied cranberry sauce
2 apples, peeled and sliced

Sauté bacon and onion together in a large skillet. When translucent, add cabbage, bay leaf, sugar, vinegar and chicken bouillon. Cook 8 minutes or until tender. Add applesauce and cranberry sauce. Mix well and simmer 5 minutes. Add apples; mix and serve.

Lisa Rubach
Elkhorn, WI

SWEET POTATO FILLED PUMPKIN

An ice cream scoop works very well for scraping out the pumpkin.

3 c. sweet potatoes, cooked
    and mashed
1/2 c. sugar
1/3 c. butter, melted
1/4 c. milk
2 eggs, beaten
1 t. vanilla extract
2-qt. size pumpkin, circular lid
    cut out and seeds and fiber
    removed

WHAT AN IDEA!

Topping:
1 c. chopped pecans
1 c. flaked coconut
1 c. brown sugar, packed
1/3 c. all-purpose flour
1/3 c. butter, melted

Combine hot sweet potatoes, sugar, butter, milk, beaten eggs and vanilla. Fill the hollowed-out pumpkin with the mixture. For topping, mix together pecans, coconut, brown sugar, flour and butter. Sprinkle over top of potato mixture. Place the filled pumpkin in a greased baking dish. Top with "lid" of pumpkin and bake for 45 minutes at 375 degrees. Remove lid and bake an additional 15 minutes or until golden brown. Allow pumpkin to cool for 10 to 15 minutes before serving.

Linda Crowley
New Albany, IN

Sweet Potato Filled Pumpkin

Genuine truly ★ old ★ fashioned Pound Cake

really truly   very good!

COUNTRY FRIENDS · SEAL OF APPROVAL

3 c. flour
1 t. baking powder
½ t. nutmeg
¼ t. salt
1½ c. butter

3 c. powdered sugar
2 t. vanilla
5 eggs
¾ c. half & half

Grease and coat with granulated sugar two 8" loaf pans or a 10" fluted tube pan.

In a bowl, combine flour, baking powder, nutmeg & salt. Set aside.

Cream together butter, powdered sugar & vanilla.

Add eggs one at a time, beating well after each addition. Mixture should be light & fluffy.

Mix in half of flour mixture until smooth. **B**lend in half & half. Beat in remaining dry ingredients until smooth.

Pour cake batter into pans. **B**ake at 350° for 45 to 75 minutes (depending on pan size) or until a wooden pick inserted in center comes out clean. Cool in pan about 10 minutes before removing.

★**Y**UMMY VARIATION: MAKE IT A CHOCOLATE CHIP POUND CAKE BY DELETING NUTMEG AND ADDING ¼ C. MINI SEMI-SWEET CHOCOLATE CHIPS!**Y**

EASY PLUM PUDDING

Pudding can be made well in advance and frozen. Reheat in the oven or by steaming.

⅓ c. butter or margarine, softened
⅔ c. brown sugar, packed
2 eggs
1 c. biscuit baking mix
2 t. orange zest, grated
¾ t. cinnamon
¾ t. nutmeg
½ c. rum, brandy or apple cider
½ c. pitted dried prunes, sliced
1 c. fine soft bread crumbs
¾ c. walnuts, chopped
1 c. applesauce
¼ t. cloves
1 c. raisins

Mix all ingredients and pour into a well greased 11½-quart mold. Cover tightly with aluminum foil and place on a rack in a large kettle. Add hot water to one-third the depth of the mold. Cover the kettle and steam the pudding for 2½ hours, adding water as necessary. Serve with Hard Sauce or Lemon Sauce.

Hard Sauce:
⅔ c. butter
2½ c. powdered sugar
enough rum to make a thick sauce

Combine ingredients.

Lemon Sauce:
½ c. sugar
1 T. cornstarch
1 c. cold water
1 T. butter
1 T. lemon juice
1 T. lemon zest, grated

Combine sugar, cornstarch and water. Bring to a boil, stirring constantly; boil for one minute. Remove from heat and stir in remaining ingredients. Makes 1¼ cups.

Diane Dollak
Fair Haven, NJ

PUMPKIN NUT ROLL
Festive and flavorful. A favorite!

3 eggs
1 c. sugar
2/3 c. canned pumpkin
1 T. lemon juice
3/4 c. all-purpose flour
1 t. baking powder
2 t. cinnamon
1 t. ginger
1 t. nutmeg
1/2 t. salt
1 c. walnuts or pecans, finely
　　chopped

Filling:
1 c. powdered sugar
2　3-oz. pkgs. cream cheese,
　　softened
1/4 c. butter, softened
1/2 t. vanilla extract

Beat the eggs for 5 minutes on high speed. Gradually add sugar. Stir in pumpkin and lemon juice. In a separate bowl, mix together flour, baking powder, cinnamon, ginger, nutmeg and salt. Fold this into the pumpkin mixture. Grease a 15"x10"x1" jelly roll pan or cookie sheet, line it with wax paper and grease the paper. Spread batter over the paper and top with the nuts. Bake at 375 degrees for 15 minutes or until done. Turn out onto a clean towel sprinkled with powdered sugar. For filling, mix together the powdered sugar, cream cheese, butter and vanilla; spread filling over the cake. Gently roll it up as for a jelly roll, using the wax paper to help push the roll. Cool and serve chilled.

Judy Borecky
Escondido, CA

Lemon Chess Pie

LEMON CHESS PIE
An old-fashioned favorite we love!

1/2 c. butter, softened
1 1/3 c. sugar
3 jumbo eggs
2 T. cornmeal
1 t. lemon extract
1 T. white vinegar
1/3 c. milk
9-inch pie crust, unbaked

Cream butter and sugar together. Stir in eggs and cornmeal. Blend in lemon extract, vinegar and milk; pour into pie crust. Bake at 350 degrees for 45 to 60 minutes or until center is set.

Ricki Treleaven
Birmingham, AL

The best thing to put in a piecrust is your teeth.

*C*lean out your pantry during the holiday season and donate extra dry and canned goods to a local food bank.

INSTRUCTIONS

BABY'S KEEPSAKE BOX

(shown on pages 8 and 9)

- 8"x10" paper maché box with clear plastic dome-insert lid
- ecru and green acrylic paint
- paintbrushes
- tracing paper
- transfer paper
- yellow, red and green fine-point paint pens
- black permanent fine-point and medium-point markers
- wood-tone spray
- clear acrylic spray sealer
- two 12-inch lengths of 1/2-inch wide satin ribbon
- hot glue gun
- fabric
- spray adhesive
- keepsakes to fit under dome

Refer to Painting Techniques, page 131, for painting tips from your Country Friends®. Allow paint, paint pens, wood-tone spray and sealer to dry after each application.

1. Remove dome insert from the lid; set aside. Paint box and lid ecru.

2. Trace the designs, page 132, onto tracing paper. Using transfer paper and repeating designs as desired, transfer baby face (one in reverse) at each side of opening in lid, leaf and berry design around opening in lid and "Baby" design on side of box.

3. Paint green stripes around sides of the lid...paint "Baby" design green. Use paint pens to paint remaining designs. Use markers to draw over transferred lines and outline stripes on the lid.

4. Apply a light coat of wood-tone spray, then 2 to 3 coats of sealer to box and lid.

5. Tie ribbons together into a bow. Glue bow to front of box.

6. Draw around cardboard insert on fabric; cut out. Apply spray adhesive to one side of the cardboard insert; smooth fabric over adhesive. Follow manufacturer's instructions to secure keepsakes under dome.

FAMILY PHOTOS BOX

(shown on page 10)

- 12 3/4-inch dia. paper maché box
- ecru, yellow, red and green acrylic paint
- paintbrushes
- photocopies of photographs (we used black and white photocopies)
- removable tape
- tracing paper
- transfer paper
- yellow and red fine-point paint pens
- black permanent fine-point and medium-point markers
- craft glue
- wood-tone spray
- clear acrylic spray sealer

Refer to Painting Techniques, page 131, for painting tips from your Country Friends®. Allow paint, paint pens, wood-tone spray, glue and sealer to dry after each application.

1. Paint lid green and box red.

2. Trim photocopies to desired sizes. Using removable tape to hold photocopies in place, arrange copies on box and lid.

3. Trace the designs, page 132, onto tracing paper. Using transfer paper and repeating designs as necessary, transfer designs to box and lid. Remove photocopies.

4. Paint ecru stripes around sides of the lid, "Family Photos" ecru and stars yellow. Use paint pens to paint the remaining designs. Use markers to draw over transferred lines and outline stripes on the lid.

5. Arrange and glue photos on the box and lid as desired.

6. Apply a light coat of wood-tone spray, then 2 to 3 coats of sealer to the box and lid.

PET FRAME

(shown on page 11)

- tracing paper
- transfer paper
- ecru photo mat (we used a 5"x7" mat with a 3"x4 1/2" opening)
- poster board
- yellow, red and black permanent fine-point markers
- wood-tone spray
- scraps of fabric
- hot glue gun
- 12-inches of black craft wire
- photograph to fit frame
- sprig of artificial greenery

1. Trace star design, page 133, onto tracing paper. Use transfer paper to transfer design to mat. Use a pencil to lightly draw pet's name on mat. Use yellow marker to color stars, red marker to color name and black marker to draw over transferred lines and outline name. Lightly spray mat with wood-tone spray; allow to dry.

2. Tear one inch wide strips of fabric one inch longer than each side of the mat opening. With 1/2-inch of strip showing through opening, glue strips to back of frame along opening edges.

3. Trace around the mat on poster board; cut out.

4. For hanger, form several loops in wire; glue ends to back of frame.

5. Center and glue photo in frame. Glue poster board to back of frame.

6. Knot a torn fabric strip around hanger; glue greenery to frame.

PET STOCKINGS

(shown on page 12)

- tracing paper
- 2 colors of felt
- 2 colors of embroidery floss

Refer to Embroidery Stitches, page 130, before beginning project. Use 3 strands of floss for all stitching unless otherwise indicated.

1. Follow *Making Patterns*, page 130, to trace patterns, page 136, onto tracing paper. For each stocking, use patterns to cut one each cuff, toe and heel from one color of felt and 2 stockings from remaining color of felt. Cut a 1"x4" strip from felt for a hanger.

2. Pin a piece of tracing paper on right side of cuff; write name on tracing paper. Using floss, work *Running Stitches* over name. Carefully remove tracing paper.

120

3. Matching edges and leaving top of stocking open, use contrasting color floss to work *Blanket Stitches* along edges to stitch stocking pieces together.

4. Matching edges, pin cuff, heel and toe to stocking front. Using floss and working through stocking front only, work *Straight Stitches* of various lengths to secure in place.

5. Fold hanger in half, insert between stocking layers, then stitch to secure.

CHRISTMAS BEARS
(shown on page 13)

ANGEL BEAR
- old-fashioned jointed Teddy bear (ours is about 14-inches tall)
- assorted fabrics
- 25-inches of 1/4-inch wide ribbon
- 2-inch wide flat cotton lace
- embroidery floss
- hot glue gun
- assorted buttons
- 5-inch dia. grapevine wreath

1. For dress, measure bear from neck to "knees" and add 2-inches. Measure around the body and triple the measurement. Cut a piece from fabric the determined measurements.

2. For casing, fold one long edge of fabric piece one inch to the wrong side and sew. Use a safety pin to thread ribbon through casing. Tie ribbon around neck to attach dress, then cut a slit in each side of the dress for arm holes.

3. For collar, measure around neck and double measurement. Cut a length of lace the determined measurement. Using 2 strands of floss, work loose *Running Stitches*, page 130, along one edge of lace. Pull floss to gather top edge of lace. Tie collar around neck.

4. For top wings, cut a 4"x25" strip from fabric. Matching wrong sides and overlapping ends one inch, fold ends of strip to the center. Tie floss tightly around overlapped area. Repeat to make bottom wings. Use floss to tie wings together; glue wings to bear.

5. Glue buttons on wreath and collar as desired. Place wreath on bear for halo.

SANTA BEAR
- assorted fabrics
- jute
- old-fashioned jointed Teddy bear (ours is about 16-inches tall)
- hot glue gun
- assorted buttons

1. For hat, tear a 13 1/2"x14" piece from one fabric for hat and a 3"x14" piece from a different fabric for cuff. Place hat fabric right side down on a flat surface. Matching one long edge, place cuff fabric right side down on hat fabric. Sew pieces together along one long edge; press piece open. Fold and press cuff up 3/4-inch, then 1 1/4-inch to the right side of hat.

2. Matching short edges and right sides, fold the hat in half. Sew edges together and turn hat right side out. Gather tip of the hat and tie a length of jute around gathers to secure. Cut clips in tip of hat to make fringe. Place hat on bear. Tie a second length of jute around hat close to bear's head.

3. Tear a 1 1/2"x24" strip from fabric and tie around bear's neck for a scarf; fringe ends. Glue buttons to hat as desired.

SANTA CLIPS
(shown on page 14)
- spring-type wooden clothespins
- white, flesh, red and black acrylic paint
- paintbrushes
- tracing paper
- transfer paper
- black permanent fine-point marker
- hot glue gun
- 1/2-inch dia. white pom-poms
- wood-tone spray

Refer to Painting Techniques, page 131, for some painting tips from your Country Friends®. Allow paint and wood-tone spray to dry after each application.

1. For each clip, take clothespin apart. Paint wooden pieces white.

2. Trace pattern, page 133, onto tracing paper. Use transfer paper to transfer design to one clothespin piece.

3. Referring to pattern for color placement and shading, paint face and hat. Use marker to add details to clip.

4. Glue pom-pom to hat. Lightly apply wood-tone spray to clothespin. Reassemble clothespin.

AUTOGRAPHED PILLOW SHAM
(shown on page 15)
- tracing paper
- transfer paper
- canvas pillow sham with flange (ours measures 18 1/2"x20" from edge to edge)
- red, green and brown embroidery floss
- paper-backed fusible web
- fabric
- washable fabric pen
- instant coffee or tea bags
- four 3/4-inch dia. buttons
- 4 each of 3/8-inch, 1/2-inch and 5/8-inch wide red heart-shaped buttons
- pillow form to fit sham

1. Trace the "All hearts come home for Christmas" design, page 133, onto tracing paper. Use transfer paper to transfer design along each edge of sham. Using 3 strands of brown floss, work *Backstitches*, page 130, over design.

2. Using the leaf pattern, page 133, follow *Making Appliqués*, page 131, to make 8 leaf and four 1 1/2"x15 1/2" strip appliqués from fabric. Overlapping ends and trimming to fit, fuse strips inside the stitched line of the flange. Arrange and fuse 2 leaves at each corner of the sham.

3. Have your Christmas time guests, grandchildren or friends that drop in use a fabric pen to sign your pillow. After everyone has signed, use 3 strands of red or green floss to work *Backstitches* over each name.

4. Refer to *Coffee or Tea Dyeing*, page 130, to dye sham. Sew one 3/4-inch dia. button at each corner of the strips. Arrange and sew one of each size heart button at each corner of sham. Place pillow form in the sham.

121

APPLE-CINNAMON WREATH
(shown on pages 16 and 17)

- 8 to 10-inch lengths of fresh pine, cedar and boxwood
- 22-gauge floral wire
- wire cutters
- 14-inch dia. wire wreath form
- 15 long cinnamon sticks
- 12 dried pomegranates
- hot glue gun
- 18 dried apple slices
- 2 yards of 3-inch wide wired ribbon

1. Bunch 2 to 3 pine lengths together; tightly wrap wire several times around one end of lengths to secure bundle. Make enough pine bundles to cover entire wreath. Covering wreath completely and overlapping as necessary, use wire to secure bundles to wreath.

2. Repeat Step 1 to make several bundles each of cedar and boxwood and cinnamon sticks. Use wire to attach bundles to wreath.

3. Insert a 20-inch length of wire through center of each pomegranate; wire pomegranates to wreath.

4. Glue 3 apple slices together in a cluster; glue to wreath as desired. Repeat to add 5 additional clusters to wreath.

5. Using ribbon, follow *Making a Bow*, page 131, to make a bow with four 8-inch loops, a center loop and two 19-inch streamers. Position, then wire bow on wreath.

WOODLAND WREATH
(shown on page 18)

- wood craft glue
- tree bark
- artificial moss
- 24-inch dia. grapevine wreath
- small artificial pine trees (we used 10 to 12-inch tall trees)
- artificial pine greenery sprigs
- 2 small artificial deer (ours are 7-inches tall)
- 2²/₃ yards of 2¹/₂-inch wide wired ribbon
- craft wire
- wire cutters
- hot glue gun

Use wood glue for all gluing unless otherwise indicated. Allow glue to dry after each application.

1. Layering as necessary, arrange and glue bark and moss on the wreath, then glue tree trunks to the bark and spot glue branches and pine greenery as necessary to secure trees in place. Arrange and glue deer on the wreath.

2. Using ribbon, follow *Making a Bow*, page 131, to make a bow with six 8-inch loops, a center loop and two 22-inch streamers. Wire bow to wreath; arrange and hot glue streamers as desired.

PINE CONE WREATH
(shown on page 19)

- preserved lemon leaves
- preserved holly leaves
- 24-inch dia. artificial pine wreath
- hot glue gun
- floral wire
- wire cutters
- pine cones
- dried red pepperberries

1. Arrange lemon and holly leaves on wreath and glue in place.

2. Using wire, attach pine cones to wreath as desired.

3. Arrange and glue pepperberries around pine cones.

SNOW-COUPLE DOOR BASKET
(shown on page 20)

- orange acrylic paint
- paintbrushes
- two 12-inch long wooden skewers
- utility scissors
- two 2¹/₂ and two 3-inch dia. plastic foam balls
- craft stick
- snow texturing medium
- whole cloves for eyes and mouth
- hot glue gun
- assorted buttons
- homespun fabric
- toddler-size socks for hats
- 4-inch long twigs
- 5"x10"x6" oval door hanging basket with flat back
- floral foam
- artificial greenery to fill basket
- natural raffia

1. Following **Steps 2 and 3** of **Snowman Topiaries**, this page, make one snow lady with earmuffs and one snowman with a hat.

2. Fill basket to 2" from the top with foam. Arrange greenery along edges of basket. Apply glue to ends of skewers on snow couple; position into the foam to secure. Arrange cedar around couple, spot glue as necessary to secure.

3. Tie several lengths of raffia into a bow around basket.

SNOWMAN TOPIARIES
(shown on pages 22 and 23)

- natural sponge
- white and orange acrylic paint
- 3-inch dia. clay flowerpots
- floral foam
- straight sticks for topiary stems (optional)
- craft stick
- snow texturing medium
- paintbrushes
- 12-inch long wooden skewers
- utility scissors
- 2¹/₂ and 3-inch dia. plastic foam balls
- whole cloves for eyes and mouth
- hot glue gun
- assorted buttons
- fabrics
- toddler-size socks for hats
- 4-inch long twigs
- artificial berry sprigs
- natural raffia
- star anise

Allow paint and snow texturing medium to dry after each application.

1. For each topiary, follow *Sponge Painting*, page 131, to sponge paint entire pot white. Fill pot with floral foam. If a stem is desired, insert a stick into the foam at center of the pot. Use a craft stick to apply snow texturing medium over foam.

2. For nose, paint one inch of pointed end of skewer orange. Cut nose from skewer. Slide one 2¹/₂-inch and one 3-inch foam ball onto remainder of skewer to form the body. Cover the body with textured snow; trim skewer. Push nose and cloves into place on face. Glue buttons on body. Tie a 1"x12" strip of fabric around snowman for a scarf.

3. Add desired headgear…For stocking cap, fold up cuff of sock leaving a floppy tip or roll up cuff to form a tight cap. Arrange and glue cap on head. For earmuffs, cut two 2-inch dia. circles from fabric. Work *Running Stitches*, page 130, along edges of circles. Pull ends of thread to tightly gather each circle; knot thread to secure. Flatten the circles with gathers at the inside center of circles. Glue one earmuff to each end of a 4-inch long twig. Arrange and glue earmuffs on snow lady. Add a sprig of artificial berries if desired.

4. Glue snowman to flowerpot or place on stem. Knot several strands of raffia around rim of pot. Glue star anise over knot in raffia.

SNOW-COUPLE BELLS
(shown on page 25)

Allow paint to dry after each application.

1. For each head, paint wooden ball white. Paint an orange nose on face. Use marker to draw eyes and mouth on face and add details to nose. Paint pink cheeks on the snow lady.

2. Cut two 6½-inch dia. circles from batting for bodies. Trace patterns, page 25, onto tracing paper. Using patterns, cut one each of hat crown, hat top and hat brim from black felt; and ear muffs from green felt.

3. For each body, use heavy thread to work *Running Stitches*, page 130, along edge of batting circle. Center bell on circle and place flowerpot over bell. Pull thread ends to gather batting over flowerpot; knot ends together to secure.

4. For each set of arms, thread wire through one cinnamon stick and button hole, then back through button and cinnamon stick; continue for opposite arm. Leaving one inch between arms, twist wire ends to secure (Fig. 1).

Fig. 1

5. Glue arms and head to top of body.

6. For snowman hat, glue short ends of hat crown together. Center and glue crown on brim; glue top on hat.

7. Glue hat on snowman, earmuffs on snow lady and remaining buttons on bodies. Tie a 1"x9" homespun scarf around each neck.

CHEERY CHAIR ORNAMENT
(continued from page 26)

2. Paint designs on chair as desired (we hand-painted dots, peppermints, trees, swirl candies, checkerboard stripes and heart designs and we stenciled the stars). Apply a light coat of wood-tone spray, then 2 to 3 coats of sealer to chair.

3. Folding fabric to fit around legs and gluing fabric edges to bottom of seat, cover seat with fabric.

SANTA CHAIR
(shown on page 27)

- wooden arm chair with removable seat
- fine-grit sand paper (optional)
- drill with ¼-inch drill bit
- 2 wooden finials
- wood glue
- two 2-inch lengths of ¼-inch dia. wooden dowel
- tack cloth
- spray primer
- white, flesh, yellow, gold, red, green and black acrylic paint
- paintbrushes
- checkerboard, star and holly leaf stencils
- wood-tone spray
- clear acrylic spray sealer
- tracing paper
- heavyweight corrugated cardboard
- polyester batting
- homespun fabric
- hot glue gun
- transfer paper
- textile medium for acrylic paint
- black permanent fine-point marker
- stapler and staples

Refer to Painting Techniques, page 131, for some painting tips from your Country Friends®. Allow glue, primer, paint, wood-tone spray and sealer to dry after each application.

1. Remove seat from chair; set aside. If necessary, sand chair to remove any peeling paint, varnish or rough spots. Drill a hole at top center of each chair back spindle and at center bottom of each finial. Use wood glue and dowel pieces to secure finials to chair. Wipe chair with a tack cloth.

2. Spray chair with primer. Paint sections of chair desired *Base Coat* colors.

3. Paint designs on chair as desired (we hand-painted dots, trees, swirl candies and checkerboard stripes, and we stenciled the checkerboard pattern along sides of seat, the stars and the holly leaves). Lightly apply wood-tone spray, then 2 to 3 coats of sealer to chair.

4. For padded chair back, trace oval pattern, page 134, onto tracing paper; cut out. Draw around pattern on cardboard, batting and wrong side of fabric. Cut out cardboard and batting along lines and fabric 2-inches outside line. Hot glue batting piece to cardboard. Center cardboard, batting side down, on wrong side of fabric. Pulling evenly and taut and clipping fabric as necessary, hot glue edges of fabric to back of cardboard.

5. Trace Santa design, page 134, onto tracing paper. Use transfer paper to transfer design to oval. Follow manufacturer's instructions to mix textile medium into paints. Referring to design for color placement, paint Santa. Use marker to outline and add details to Santa.

6. To cover seat of chair, draw around seat on wrong side of fabric; cut out 4 inches outside drawn lines. Cut a piece from batting the same size as fabric piece. Layer batting, then seat at center on wrong side of fabric. Fold fabric and batting diagonally over seat corners; staple to secure. Alternating sides and pulling taut, staple edges of fabric to bottom of seat; trim as necessary. Reattach seat to chair.

CROSS-STITCHED PILLOWS
(continued from page 28)

2. Referring to **Santa or Reindeer Diagram**, sew strips to stitched piece in numerical order, trimming strips even with piece as you go.

Santa Diagram ### Reindeer Diagram

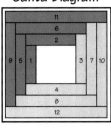 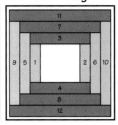

3. Follow **Pillow Finishing** to complete the pillow.

Snowman Pillow Top

1. Cut four 2¹/₂"x6¹/₄" pieces from red fabric and four 2¹/₂" squares from green fabric.

2. Sew one red piece to top and bottom of stitched piece. For side borders, sew a green square to each end of each remaining red piece; sew borders to sides of pillow top.

3. Follow **Pillow Finishing** to complete the pillow.

Pillow Finishing

1. For embroidered stars, trace star pattern, page 138, onto stencil plastic; cut out. Using quilt marking pencil, mark stars on pillow top as desired. Using 3 strands of yellow floss, work *Running Stitches* over stars.

2. Cut a piece from fabric the same size as pillow top for pillow back.

3. For welting, measure around edges of pillow top; add 4-inches. Cut a bias strip from fabric 2-inches wide by the determined measurement (piecing as necessary). Cut a piece of cord the determined measurement.

4. Press one end of strip ¹/₂-inch to wrong side. Beginning ¹/₂-inch from pressed end, center cord on wrong side of strip. Fold strip over cord. Beginning ¹/₂-inch from pressed end, use a zipper foot to baste close to cord along length of strip. Trim seam allowance to ¹/₄-inch.

5. Beginning with pressed end of welting and matching raw edges, pin welting to right side of pillow top (Fig.1). Trimming to fit, insert unfinished end of welting into folded end of welting (Fig. 2). Using a zipper foot, baste welting in place close to cord.

Fig. 1

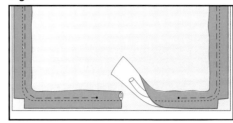

Fig. 2

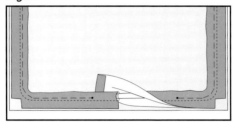

6. Matching right sides and leaving an opening for turning, sew pillow top and pillow back together. Clip corners and turn right side out. Stuff pillow with fiberfill and sew opening closed.

SANTA WALL HANGING
(shown on page 30)

- embroidery floss (see color key, page 139)
- 10¹/₂-inch square of Klostern
- assorted red and green fabrics
- polyester batting
- stencil plastic
- quilt marking pencil

Refer to Cross Stitch, page 130, and separate and realign floss strands before stitching. For all sewing, match right sides and raw edges, use a ¹/₄-inch seam allowance and trim strips even with wall hanging unless otherwise indicated.

1. Using 9 strands of floss for *Cross Stitches*, 3 strands of floss for *Backstitches* and 4 strands of floss for *French Knots*, center and stitch Santa design, page 139, on Klostern.

2. Wash, dry and press fabrics. Cut 10 red and 10 green 2"x26" strips from fabrics. For wall hanging top, refer to **Wall Hanging Diagram** to sew strips to stitched piece in numerical order.

Wall Hanging Diagram

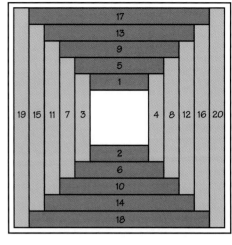

3. Cut one piece each from batting and fabric for backing the same size as wall hanging front. Place backing wrong side up on a flat surface. Layer batting, then wall hanging top right side up on backing. Use safety pins to pin-baste layers together.

4. Trace star pattern, page 139, onto stencil plastic; cut out. Using quilt marking pencil, mark stars around fabric border as desired. Using yellow floss, work *Running Stitches*, page 130, around each star through all layers; remove pins.

5. Cut a 7"x25" strip from fabric for hanging sleeve. Press ends ¹/₄-inch to wrong side, press ¹/₄-inch to wrong side again and sew in place. Matching wrong sides and long edges, press strip in half. Matching raw edges, pin hanging sleeve to center top edge on back of wall hanging.

6. Cut four 1¹/₂"x26" binding strips. Matching wrong sides and long edges, press each strip in half. Matching raw edges, center and sew a strip to top and bottom of wall hanging; trim ends even with edges of wall hanging. Fold binding over to backing covering stitch line; pin in place. Hand stitch binding to backing.

7. Center and sew remaining strips to sides of wall hanging. Trim each end ¹/₂-inch longer than bound edge. Fold ends to back and stitch in place. Fold binding over to backing and hand stitch in place.

8. Hand stitch bottom of hanging sleeve to back of quilt.

REINDEER FEED BAG

(continued from page 31)

2. Matching right sides and short edges, fold Klostern in half; sew edges together, forming a tube. Fold tube with seam at center back. Sew bottom edges of bag together…finger press sides of bag.

3. For each bottom corner, match pressed side seam to bottom seam and sew across corner 2-inches from point (Fig. 1).

Fig. 1

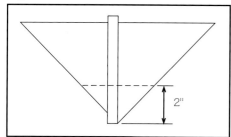

2"

4. Fold top of bag 2-inches to wrong side; stitch to secure. Turn bag right side out.

5. Place gift in bag. Arrange twigs, apple picks and juniper together into a bundle; use floral tape to secure bundle. Tuck ends of bundle into top of bag. Tie ribbon into a bow around top of bag.

STAR PLACE CARD

(shown on page 32)

- ecru card stock
- paper-backed fusible web
- fabric scraps
- hot glue gun
- 3/4-inch dia. red button
- black permanent fine-point marker

1. For each place card, cut a 2"x4" piece from card stock.

2. Using small star pattern, page 140, follow Making Appliqués, page 131, to make one star appliqué and 2 each 1/2"x2" and 1/2"x4" strip appliqués from fabric scraps. Arrange and fuse strips and star on place card.

3. Glue button to center of star. Use marker to draw "stitches" along edges of strips and write name on card.

STAR NAPKIN RING & NAPKIN

(shown on page 32)

- paper-backed fusible web
- fabric scraps
- poster board
- hot glue gun
- 1/2-inch dia. green button
- 3/4-inch dia. red button
- pinking shears
- fabric for napkins

1. For each napkin ring, use the large star pattern, page 140, and follow Making Appliqués, page 131, to make one star appliqué from fabric scraps. Fuse star to poster board; cut out.

2. Make one 2"x6" strip appliqué from fabric scraps; do not remove paper backing. Press each long edge 1/2-inch to wrong side. Remove paper backing, refold and fuse in place.

3. Overlap ends of strip 1/2-inch and glue to secure. Glue star over overlapped ends; glue buttons to center of star.

4. For each napkin, use pinking shears to cut a 17-inch square from fabric for napkins.

SNOWMAN TABLE RUNNER

(shown on page 33)

- 21"x65" fabric piece for backing (this will be your outer border, too)
- 1/2-inch wide fusible web tape
- 16"x60" fabric piece for top
- paper-backed fusible web
- fabric scraps for appliqués
- black permanent fine-point marker
- hot glue gun
- seven 3/4-inch dia. red buttons

1. Cut a 2 1/2-inch square from each corner of backing fabric. Fuse a length of web tape along each edge on wrong side of backing fabric…do not remove paper backing.

2. Fuse a length of web tape along each edge on wrong side of top fabric piece. Center and fuse top fabric piece on wrong side of backing fabric piece.

3. Overlap and press backing fabric edges over top fabric piece. Remove paper backing from backing fabric. Fold and fuse long edges, then short edges to front of runner.

4. Using patterns, page 140, follow Making Appliqués, page 131, to make one snowman appliqué; 2 each (one each in reverse) arm, sock, toe, heel and cuff appliqués and 4 small star appliqués from fabric scraps. Make one 7 1/2"x11 1/2" background appliqué, 2 each 1/2"x13" and 1/2"x57 1/2" border appliqués and eleven 1"x4" strip appliqués from fabric.

5. Overlapping ends, fuse short, then long border appliqués to runner. Center and fuse background at one end of runner. Matching edges and trimming to fit, fuse strip appliqués along edges of background. Arrange and fuse remaining appliqués on background.

6. Use marker to draw "blanket stitches" along edges of snowman and draw eyes and mouth on face. Glue buttons to snowman and stars. Knot a 3/4"x2" strip of fabric at center; glue to snowman for scarf.

TINY STOCKING & STAR TREE

(shown on page 33)

- paper-backed fusible web
- assorted fabrics
- poster board
- tracing paper
- white, red and green pony beads
- cotton string
- 12-inch tall artificial tree
- hot glue gun
- drawing compass
- pinking shears

1. Fuse fabric for stockings and stars to poster board.

2. Trace stocking and star patterns, page 140, onto tracing paper. Draw around stocking (draw around some in reverse) and star patterns on wrong side of fabric-covered poster board desired number of times; cut out shapes.

3. Using cuff, heel and toe patterns, page 140, follow Making Appliqués, page 131, to make one each cuff, heel and toe appliqué for each stocking from fabric…remember to make reversed appliqués for reversed stockings. Arrange and fuse appliqués on stockings.

4. For garland, thread beads onto string to desired length; knot string ends to secure.

5. For bows, tear 3/4"x10" strips from fabric. Tie each strip into a bow. Arrange bows, garland, stockings and stars on tree; glue to secure.

6. For tree skirt, use compass to draw and pinking shears to cut a 10-inch dia. circle from fabric; cut a 3/4-inch dia. circle at center of circle. For skirt opening, cut skirt from center circle to outer edge of circle; arrange around bottom of tree.

NATURALS TABLETOP TREE
(shown on page 37)

- raffia
- 3-inch long cinnamon sticks
- hot glue gun
- star anise
- homespun fabrics
- dried apple slices
- wire cutters
- craft wire
- utility scissors
- small pine cones
- small candles
- grapefruits or oranges
- small cookie cutters
- whole cloves
- small pomegranates
- red acrylic paint
- paintbrush
- one, 2 and 3-inch long oval Shaker boxes with lids
- dried bay leaves
- 3-foot tall artificial tree "planted" in a wicker basket

1. For garland, thread raffia through cinnamon sticks. (If you have difficulty threading raffia through the cinnamon sticks, soak the sticks in water until they uncurl slightly.) Glue one star anise to raffia between each cinnamon stick; knot ends of raffia to secure.

2. For each apple slice ornament, tear a 1"x8" strip from fabric; tie into a bow. For hanger, bend 4-inches of wire into a "U" shape. Glue ends of wire to apple slice; glue bow over ends of wire.

3. For each candle ornament, use utility scissors to cut 2-inches from bottom of pine cone; discard top. Glue candle in pine cone. Tie several 9-inch lengths of raffia into a bow; glue to pine cone.

4. Refer to page 40 to make several **Citrus Peel Cut-outs**. Insert a 4-inch length of wire through the top of each cut-out; curl wire ends.

5. For each pomegranate basket, glue cloves to top of pomegranate. For hanger, bend 4-inches of wire into a "U" shape; glue ends to pomegranate.

6. For each painted box ornament, paint box and lid red; allow to dry. Place lid on box. Knot several strands of raffia around box. Glue one bay leaf under knot and one star anise over knot of raffia.

7. For tree topper, arrange 5 cinnamon sticks into a star shape; glue cinnamon sticks at center to secure. Arrange and glue 5 bay leaves over cinnamon sticks. Glue one star anise at center of bay leaves. Glue center of an 8-inch length of wire to back of topper.

8. Arrange garland on tree. Glue candle and box ornaments and hang remaining ornaments on tree. Wire topper to tree. Tie a fabric bow at top of tree and around basket.

TREE-TOPPER STAR
(shown on page 44)

- tracing paper
- pinking shears
- paper-backed fusible web
- 3 homespun fabrics
- tracing paper
- green embroidery floss
- assorted colors and sizes of buttons
- polyester fiberfill
- 10-inches of craft wire

1. Using patterns, page 142, follow *Making Patterns*, page 130, to make whole large star, small star and heart patterns. Using pinking shears and small star and heart patterns, follow *Making Appliqués*, page 131, to make one star and one heart appliqué from fabrics. Using pattern, cut 2 large stars from remaining fabric.

2. Center and fuse star and heart appliqués on right side of one large star. Using 6 strands of floss, work *Running Stitches*, page 130, along edges of appliquéd star. Sew buttons to star and heart appliqués as desired.

3. Matching wrong sides, using a 1/4-inch seam allowance and leaving an opening for turning, sew large stars together. Turn star right side out and stuff with fiberfill; sew opening closed.

4. Tack center of wire to back of tree topper for hanger.

BUTTON TREE SKIRT
(shown on page 46)

- 1 1/3 yards of 44"w red checked fabric
- string
- chalk pencil
- thumbtack
- pinking shears
- 1 2/3 yards of 54"w green fabric
- green embroidery floss
- paper-backed fusible web
- red fabric scraps
- assorted buttons

1. Matching right sides, fold red fabric in half from top to bottom and again from left to right.

2. Tie one end of string to chalk pencil. Insert thumbtack through string 22-inches from the pencil. Insert thumbtack through the fabric as shown in Fig. 1; mark the outside cutting line.

Fig. 1

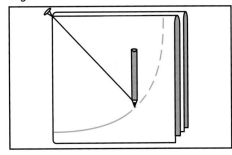

3. Repeat Step 2, inserting thumbtack 2-inches from the pencil; mark the inner cutting line. Use pinking shears to cut along drawn lines through all layers of fabric.

4. Using 26-inches for outer cutting line and 2-inches for inner cutting line, repeat Steps 1-3 to make a liner from green fabric.

5. Center and pin red circle on liner. Draw a straight line from inner circle to outer edge of liner for skirt opening.

6. Using 6 strands of floss, work *Running Stitches*, page 130, ½-inch inside edges of red circle and along both sides of drawn line to secure pieces together. Use pinking shears to cut along opening line.

7. Using pinking shears and pattern, page 142, follow *Making Appliqués*, page 131, to make desired number of heart appliqués from fabric scraps. Arrange and fuse hearts on skirt. Sew buttons on skirt as desired.

BUTTON LAMP
(continued from page 50)

3. Center and fuse tree and 2 stars on fabric piece…fuse remaining stars near ends of piece. Using yellow floss, work *Blanket Stitches* along edges of tree. Using green floss, work *Running Stitches* along edges of stars. Sew buttons to tree and center of stars. Work green *Straight Stitches* around button on each star. Follow manufacturer's instructions to cover shade with fabric. Glue additional buttons to shade as desired.

4. For trim along top edge of shade, cut a 1½"x14½" bias strip from trim fabric. Matching right sides and long edges, press strip in half. Inserting top of shade in fold of strip and overlapping ends at back of shade, glue strip around top edge. Using pinking shears to cut strip, repeat to add a 1½"x35½" bias strip to bottom edge of shade.

5. Fill jar with buttons. Follow manufacturer's instructions to place lamp on jar. Place jar in wire jar holder and shade on lamp.

BUTTON PHOTO ALBUM
(shown on page 51)

- photo album with center rings
- homespun fabric
- spray adhesive
- hot glue gun
- pinking shears
- pre-cut photo mat to fit on album cover
- photograph to fit in mat
- assorted buttons

1. To cover album, draw around open album on wrong side of fabric; cut out fabric 2-inches outside drawn lines. Apply spray adhesive to wrong side of fabric; center open album on fabric. Close album; smooth fabric on front and back of album. Re-open album…fold corners of fabric diagonally over corners of album. Clipping top and bottom edges to fit under binding hardware, fold edges of fabric over edges of album; hot glue corners if necessary.

2. To cover inside of album, measure height of front cover; subtract ½-inch. Measure width of front cover. Use pinking shears to cut 2 pieces from fabric the determined measurements.

3. Apply spray adhesive to wrong sides of fabric pieces. Placing side edge under binding hardware, center and smooth fabric pieces to inside front and back of album.

4. Leaving top edge open, hot glue outside edges of mat to center front of album.

5. Allowing buttons to extend over edges of mat, hot glue one layer of buttons over front of mat. Continue gluing buttons on top of first layer as desired. Place photograph in frame.

RAGGEDY SUZANNE
(shown on page 60)

- tracing paper
- transfer paper
- 22-inch tall muslin doll
- white, red and black acrylic paint
- paintbrushes
- black permanent fine-point marker
- polyurethane semi-gloss varnish
- red cotton knit doll hair loops
- 1½"x16" torn fabric strip
- two 8-inch square red-and-white-striped fabric pieces
- hot glue gun
- plaid fabric for dress
- small sew-on snaps
- muslin
- assorted buttons
- paper-backed fusible web
- fabric scraps for appliqués

Allow paint and varnish to dry after each application. Match right sides and raw edges and use a ¼-inch seam allowance for all stitching unless otherwise indicated.

1. Trace face pattern, page 135, onto tracing paper. Use transfer paper to transfer face to center of muslin doll head. Paint face on doll. Use marker to outline eyes.

2. For shoes, paint doll's feet black. Apply 2 to 3 coats of varnish to shoes.

3. Tack hair loops to head. Tie torn fabric strip into a bow, then tack bow to head.

4. For each stocking, press edges of striped squares ¼-inch to wrong side. Matching one edge with top of shoe and overlapping edges at back, wrap stocking around leg. Catching leg in stitching, stitch back seam to secure. Glue edge above shoe to secure.

5. Use tracing paper and refer to **Bodice Diagram**, to make bodice pattern. For bodice, cut a 10"x21" piece from plaid fabric. Matching long edges, fold fabric in half. Aligning shoulders of bodice pattern with fold of fabric, cut out bodice. For back opening, unfold and cut bodice down center back. Press each raw edge of back opening ¼-inch to wrong side, repeat and sew in place.

Bodice Diagram

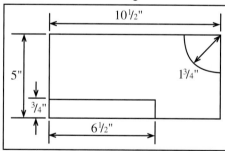

6. For ruffle, cut a 2"x24" strip from plaid fabric. Press ends ¼-inch to wrong side. Matching wrong sides and long edges, baste ¼-inch from raw edges. Gather ruffle to fit neck; pin in place. Sew ruffle to dress. Press seam allowance to wrong side; topstitch in place.

7. Press raw edges of sleeves ¼-inch to wrong side; repeat and sew in place. Sew underarm and side seams.

8. For skirt, cut a 10"x45" piece from plaid fabric. For hem, press one long edge ¼-inch, then ½-inch to the wrong side; stitch in place. For skirt back opening, press each short edge ¼-inch to wrong side; repeat and sew in place. Baste ¼-inch from raw edge. Pull basting threads, gathering skirt to fit bottom edge of bodice; pin in place. Sew skirt to bodice. Stitch snaps along back of dress opening. Place dress on doll.

9. For apron, cut a 17"x20" piece from muslin. Press short edges ¼-inch to wrong side. Matching right sides and long edges, fold apron in half. Sew long edges together (top). Turn right side out; press. Topstitch along side edges.

10. For apron tie, cut a 2½"x42" strip from muslin. Press each edge ¼-inch to wrong side. Matching wrong sides and long edges, fold strip in half. Topstitch along pressed edges. Repeat using 2½"x6" strips to make shoulder straps.

11. Baste 1½-inch from top of apron. Pull basting threads, drawing up gathers to measure 7½-inches. Centering apron tie over gathers on right side of apron, topstitch tie to apron.

12. Place apron on doll. Pin to mark straps in place on apron. Remove apron and sew straps in place. Stitch buttons to apron.

13. Using patterns, page 135, follow Making Appliqués, page 131, to make 3 each tree and trunk appliqués from fabric scraps. Arrange and fuse appliqués on apron.

SOCK GINGERBOY
(shown on page 60)
- 2 men's brown work socks
- tracing paper
- polyester fiberfill
- heavy thread
- dark red felt
- 5 black buttons

1. Cut cuff and toe from each sock; set aside. Cut socks open along heel side.

2. Using pattern, page 146, follow Making Patterns, page 130, to draw whole gingerboy pattern onto tracing paper; cut out. Matching right sides, place sock pieces together. Pin pattern to socks. Leaving an opening for turning, sew along pattern line; cut out ¼-inch outside sewn line. Carefully remove pattern. Turn right side out…stuff with fiberfill. Stitch opening closed.

3. For hat, tightly wrap and tie heavy thread around cut edge of cuff…turn right side out. For pom-pom, cut two 1"x2" pieces from felt. Stack pieces on top of each other; tie thread tightly around center of pieces to secure. Cut fringes in ends of pieces. Stitch pom-pom to top of hat. Turn brim of hat up two times and place on gingerboy.

4. Sew buttons to gingerboy. For bow tie, cut a ¾"x1¾" piece from felt. Tie thread tightly around center of piece to gather; stitch bow tie to gingerboy.

FLEECE MITTENS
(shown on page 65)
- tracing paper
- green polar fleece
- ecru, red and gold felt
- pinking shears
- assorted embroidery floss
- two ½-inch dia. buttons
- two 8-inch lengths of ⅜-inch wide elastic

Refer to Embroidery Stitches, page 130, before beginning projects. Use 3 strands of floss for stitches unless otherwise indicated.

1. Using patterns, page 147, follow Making Patterns, page 130, to make a whole mitten pattern and one star pattern. Using patterns, cut 2 stars from gold felt and 4 mitten shapes from fleece. Cut two ¾"x10" strips for casings and two 1½-inch squares from red felt. Using pinking shears, cut two 2-inch squares from ecru felt.

2. For each mitten, leaving mitten open at wrist, use a ½-inch seam allowance to sew 2 mitten shapes together. Turn mitten right side out. Arrange and pin squares, then star on front of mitten. Stitching through front layer only, use

floss to work Blanket Stitches along edges of red square and Running Stitches along edges of star. Sew one button at center of star.

3. For elastic casing, beginning at thumb seam, pin red strip around mitten one inch from open edge. Work Running Stitches along long edges of strip. Use a safety pin to insert elastic through casing. Overlap elastic ends ¼-inch; sew ends together. Stitch casing closed.

FRIENDSHIP SAMPLER
(shown on page 68)
- 8"x10" unfinished wooden frame
- green acrylic paint
- paintbrush
- wood-tone spray
- scraps of assorted fabrics
- hot glue gun
- muslin
- instant coffee or tea bags
- tracing paper
- embroidery floss
- pinking shears
- paper-backed fusible web
- assorted buttons
- corrugated cardboard
- spray adhesive
- kraft paper

Refer to Embroidery Stitches, page 130, for some tips from your Country Friends®. Use 3 strands of floss for all stitching.

1. Paint frame green; allow to dry. Lightly apply wood-tone spray to frame; allow to dry.

2. Adjusting strips to fit, knot torn 1"x6" strips from fabric scraps together and hot glue to frame…trim ends of strips as necessary.

3. Cut two 11"x14" pieces from muslin. Refer to Coffee or Tea Dyeing, page 130, to dye muslin. Matching edges, baste pieces together along outer edges.

4. Trace friendship pattern, page 152, onto tracing paper. Center and pin pattern on basted muslin piece. Stitching through paper, work red French Knots for berries, green Straight Stitches for pine needles and black Running Stitches for words. Carefully remove paper.

5. Using pinking shears and heart pattern, page 152, follow *Making Appliqués*, page 131, to make 3 heart appliqués from fabric scraps; fuse hearts to stitched piece. Work *Running Stitches* on hearts along edges; sew a button to center of each heart.

6. Cut a piece from cardboard to fit in frame. Apply spray adhesive to wrong side of stitched piece; center and smooth onto cardboard piece…wrap edges to back of cardboard. Hot glue stitched piece in frame.

7. Draw around frame on kraft paper; cut out 1/4-inch inside drawn line. Hot glue paper over back of frame.

SNOWMAN BOX

(shown on page 70)
- white, blue and green acrylic paint
- paintbrushes
- 6-inch dia. Shaker box with lid
- tracing paper
- transfer paper
- black permanent fine-point marker
- wood-tone spray
- clear acrylic spray sealer

Refer to Painting Techniques, page 131, before beginning project. Allow paint, wood-tone spray and sealer to dry after each application.

1. Paint top of lid blue. Paint sides of lid and entire box green. Paint faint white lines down sides of lid and box.

2. Trace pattern, page 141, onto tracing paper. Use transfer paper to transfer design to lid. Use marker to draw over transferred lines. Referring to pattern for color placement, paint snowman. Paint white "snowflakes" around snowman. Use marker to draw over transferred lines again.

3. Lightly dry brush lid and box white. Lightly apply wood-tone spray, then 2 to 3 coats of sealer to box and lid.

YO-YO COOKIE JARS

(shown on pages 72 and 73)
- jars with lids
- drawing compass
- tracing paper
- homespun fabrics
- heavy thread
- hot glue gun
- assorted buttons
- Christmasy colors of acrylic paint
- paintbrushes
- wooden cut-outs
- black permanent fine-point marker
- jute
- wooden spools (optional)

1. For each yo-yo, measure across jar lid; double the measurement and add 1/4-inch. Measuring between compass point and pencil, adjust compass to the determined measurement; draw a circle on tracing paper, then cut out for pattern. Using pattern, cut circle from fabric.

2. Press raw edge of circle 1/4-inch to the wrong side. Using heavy thread, work loose *Running Stitches*, page 130, along pressed edge. Pull ends of thread to tightly gather the circle; knot thread to secure. Flatten circle with gathers at top center. Glue flat side of yo-yo to top of lid; glue a button to center of gathers on yo-yo.

3. Paint cut-outs; allow to dry. Use marker to draw "stitches" along edges of cut-outs. Glue buttons on cut-outs if desired.

4. Measure around neck of jar; add 10-inches. Cut a length of jute the determined measurement. Glue buttons, cut-outs or spools to jute as desired; loosely tie jute around neck of jar.

GIFT CANISTERS

(shown on page 79)
- hammer
- nail
- assorted tin cans (labels removed)
- spray primer
- desired colors of acrylic paint
- paintbrushes
- foam paintbrush
- acrylic stain
- black fine-point paint pen
- clear matte water-based polyurethane sealer
- black craft wire
- paper-backed fusible web
- fabric scraps
- poster board
- hot glue gun

Allow primer, paint, paint pen and sealer to dry after each application.

1. For each canister, use hammer and nail to punch one hole on each side of can below top rim.

2. Spray outside of can with primer, then paint desired color. Use foam paintbrush to apply a light coat of stain to outside of can; quickly remove excess stain with a soft rag.

3. Use pen to draw "stitches" along top and bottom rims of cans. Apply 2 to 3 coats of sealer to canister.

4. For handle, thread ends of desired length of wire through holes in canister; twist wire around itself to secure.

5. Using the patterns, page 135, follow *Making Appliqués*, page 131, to make desired appliqués from fabrics. Arrange and fuse appliqués on poster board, then cut out. Embellish appliqués with buttons, bows or a message, then glue to canister.

MITTEN COASTERS

(shown on page 82)
- tracing paper
- red felt
- cotton batting
- white and black embroidery floss
- fabric for cuffs
- paper-backed fusible web
- pinking shears
- hot glue gun
- 3/4-inch dia. buttons

1. Trace mitten pattern, page 151, onto tracing paper. For each coaster, use pattern to cut 2 mittens from felt and one mitten (1/8-inch larger) from batting. Layer batting mitten between felt mittens. Using 3 strands of white floss, work *Running Stitches*, page 130, along edges of mitten to secure.

2. For cuff, cut one 2 3/4"x3 3/4" piece each from fabric, batting and web. Fuse fabric to batting; use pinking shears to trim short edges. Using 3 strands of black floss, work *Running Stitches* along one pinked edge. Matching short edges, press cuff in half. With stitched edge at front, glue top of mitten between folds of cuff. Knotting floss at front, sew button to outer corner of cuff.

GENERALS

COFFEE OR TEA DYEING

Coffee Dying: Dissolve 2 tablespoons instant coffee in 2 cups of hot water; allow to cool.

Tea Dying: Steep one tea bag in 2 cups of hot water; allow to cool.

For Both: Immerse fabric or lace into coffee or tea. Soak until desired color is achieved. Remove from coffee or tea and allow to dry. Press if desired.

CROSS STITCH

Preparing floss: If your project will be laundered, soak floss in a mixture of one cup water and one tablespoon vinegar for a few minutes and allow to dry before using to prevent colors from bleeding or fading.

Counted Cross Stitch (X): Work one Cross Stitch to correspond to each colored square in chart. For horizontal rows, work stitches in two journeys.

Fig. 1

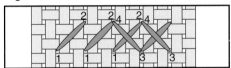

For vertical rows, complete stitch as shown.

Fig. 2

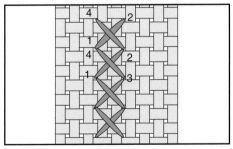

When working over 2 fabric threads, work Cross Stitch as shown.

Fig. 3

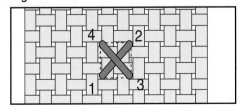

Backstitch (B'ST): For outline detail, Backstitch (shown in chart and color key by black or colored straight lines) should be worked after all Cross Stitch has been completed.

Fig. 4

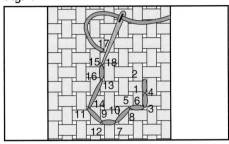

EMBROIDERY STITCHES

Preparing floss: If your project will be laundered, soak floss in a mixture of one cup water and one tablespoon vinegar for a few minutes and allow to dry before using to prevent colors from bleeding or fading.

Backstitch: Referring to Fig. 1, bring needle up at 1; go down at 2; bring up at 3 and pull through. For next stitch, insert needle at 1; bring up at 4 and pull through.

Fig. 1

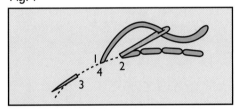

Blanket Stitch: Referring to Fig. 2a, bring needle up at 1. Keeping thread below point of needle, go down at 2 and come up at 3. Continue working as shown in Fig. 2b.

Fig. 2a   **Fig. 2b**

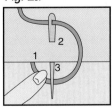   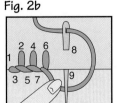

French Knot: Referring to Fig. 3, bring needle up at 1. Wrap floss once around needle and insert needle at 2, holding end of floss with non-stitching fingers.

Tighten knot, then pull needle through fabric, holding floss until it must be released. For a larger knot, use more strands; wrap only once.

Fig. 3

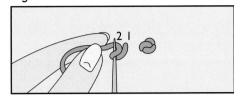

Lazy Daisy Stitch: Bring needle up at 1; take needle down again at 1 to form a loop and bring up at 2. Keeping loop below point of needle (Fig. 4), take needle down at 3 to anchor loop.

Fig. 4

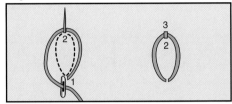

Running Stitch: Referring to Fig. 5, make a series of straight stitches with stitch length equal to the space between stitches.

Fig. 5

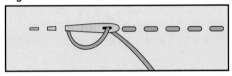

Straight Stitch: Referring to Fig. 6, come up at 1 and go down at 2.

Fig. 6

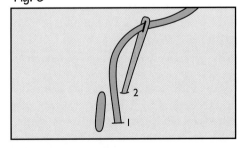

MAKING PATTERNS

When the entire pattern is shown, place tracing paper over the pattern and draw over lines. For a more durable pattern, use a permanent marker to draw over pattern on stencil plastic.

When patterns are stacked or overlapped, place tracing paper over the pattern and follow a single colored line to trace the pattern. Repeat to trace each pattern separately onto tracing paper.

When tracing a two-part pattern, match the dashed lines and arrows to trace the pattern onto tracing paper.

When only half of the pattern is shown (indicated by a solid blue line on pattern), fold the tracing paper in half. Place the fold along the solid blue line and trace pattern half; turn folded paper over and draw over the traced lines on the remaining side. Unfold the pattern; cut out.

MAKING APPLIQUÉS

To prevent darker fabrics from showing through, white or light-colored fabrics may need to be lined with fusible interfacing before being fused.

To make reverse appliqués, trace the pattern onto tracing paper; turn traced paper over and continue to follow all steps using the reversed pattern.

1. Trace the appliqué pattern onto paper side of web as many times as indicated for a single fabric. When making more than one appliqué, leave at least one inch between shapes.

2. Cutting 1/2-inch outside drawn shape, cut out web shape. Fuse to wrong side of fabric.

3. Cut out the appliqué shape along the drawn lines.

MAKING A BOW

Note: Loop sizes given in project instructions refer to the length of ribbon used to make one loop of bow.

1. For first streamer, measure desired length of streamer from one end of ribbon; twist ribbon between fingers as shown in Fig. 1.

Fig. 1

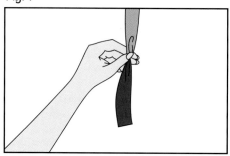

2. Keeping right side of ribbon facing out, fold ribbon to front to form desired-size loop; gather ribbon between fingers (Fig. 2). Fold ribbon to back to form another loop; gather ribbon between fingers (Fig. 3).

Fig. 2

Fig. 3

3. If a center loop is desired, form half the desired number of loops, then loosely wrap ribbon around thumb and gather ribbon between fingers as shown in Fig. 4; form remaining loops. Continue to form loops, varying size of loops as desired, until bow is desired size.

Fig. 4

4. For remaining streamer, trim ribbon to desired length.

5. To secure bow, hold gathered loops tightly. Fold a length of floral wire around gathers of loops. Hold wire ends behind bow, gathering all loops forward; twist bow to tighten wire. Arrange loops and trim ribbon ends as desired.

PAINTING TECHNIQUES

Transferring a pattern: Trace pattern onto tracing paper. Place transfer paper coated side down between project and traced pattern. Use removable tape to secure pattern to project. Use a pencil to draw over outlines of design (press lightly to avoid smudges and heavy lines that are difficult to cover). If necessary, use a soft eraser to remove any smudges.

Painting base coats: Use a medium round brush for large areas and a small round brush for small areas. Do not overload brush. Allowing to dry between coats, apply several thin coats of paint to project.

Transferring details: To transfer detail lines to design, reposition pattern and transfer paper over painted base coats and use a pencil to lightly draw over detail lines of design.

Adding details: Use a permanent marker or paint pen to draw over detail lines.

Sealing: If an item will be handled frequently or used outdoors, we recommend sealing the item with clear acrylic sealer. Sealers are available in spray or brush-on form in several finishes. Follow the manufacturer's instructions to apply the sealer.

Shading and highlighting: Dip one corner of a flat brush in water; blot on a paper towel. Dip dry corner of brush into paint. Stroke brush back and forth on palette until there is a gradual change from paint to water in each brush stroke. Stroke loaded side of brush along detail line on project, pulling brush toward you and turning project if necessary. For shading, side load brush with a darker color of paint. For highlighting, side load brush with lighter color of paint.

Spatter Painting: Dip the bristle tips of a dry toothbrush into paint, blot on a paper towel to remove excess, then pull thumb across bristles to spatter paint on project.

Sponge Painting: Use an assembly-line method when making several sponge-painted projects. Place project on a covered work surface. Practice sponge-painting technique on scrap paper until desired look is achieved. Paint projects with first color and allow to dry before moving to next color. Use a clean sponge for each additional color.

For allover designs, dip a dampened sponge piece into paint; remove excess paint on a paper towel. Use a light stamping motion to paint item.

For painting with sponge shapes, dip a dampened sponge shape into paint; remove excess paint on a paper towel. Lightly press sponge shape onto project. Carefully lift sponge. For a reverse design, turn sponge shape over.

Baby

baby face

star sprig

star

leaf & berry

FAMILY PHOTOS BOX
(page 10)

Family
Photos

PET FRAME
(page 11)

AUTOGRAPHED PILLOW SHAM
(page 15)

SANTA CLIPS
(page 14)

STAR & WREATH ORNAMENTS
(page 45)

All Hearts Come Home For Christmas

SANTA CHAIR
(page 27)

GIFT CANISTERS
(page 78)

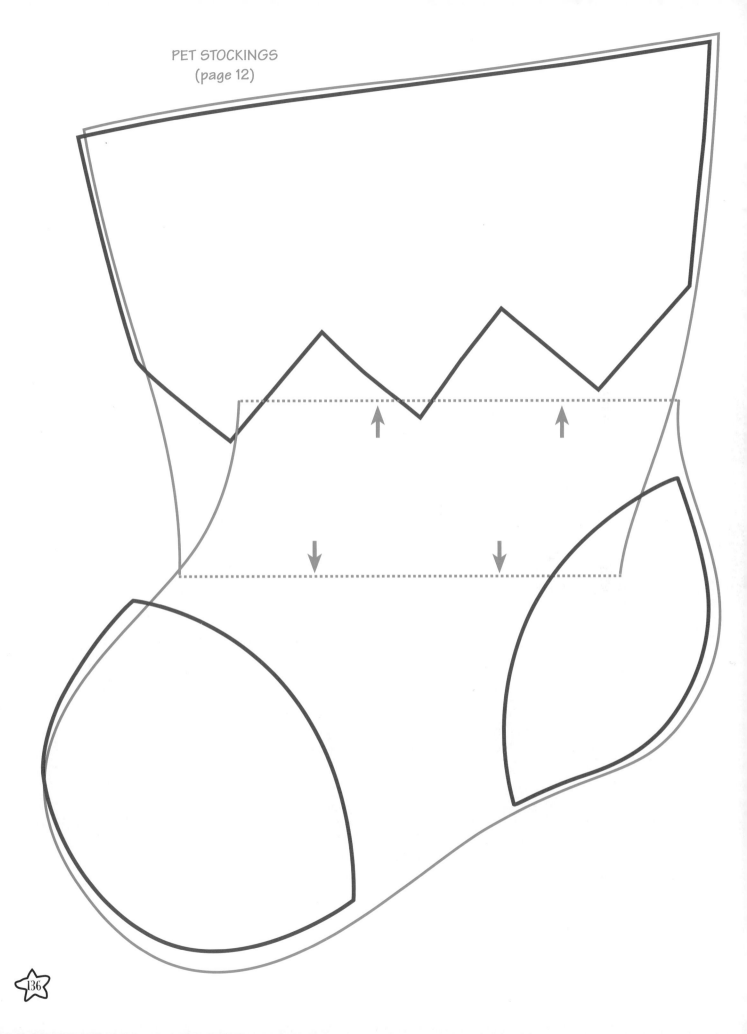

PET STOCKINGS
(page 12)

136

Snowman (67w x 67h)

X	DMC	ANC.	X	DMC	ANC.	X	DMC	B'ST	ANC.
·	blanc	2	2	721	925	$	959		186
●	304	1006	✕	762	234	Σ	3371	／	382
◆	318	399	∅	806	169	●	3746		1030
✔	321	9046	▫	813	161	◇	3747		120
T	341	117	◈	822	390	¢	3820		306
>	415	398	✖	824	164	V	3822		295
▲	435	1046	◉	826	161	●	blanc		2 Fr. Knot
✚	436	1045	✤	910	229	●	910		229 Fr. Knot
%	605	1094	▽	912	209	●	3371		382 Fr. Knot
4	720	326	⊠	958	187	●	3821		305 Fr. Knot

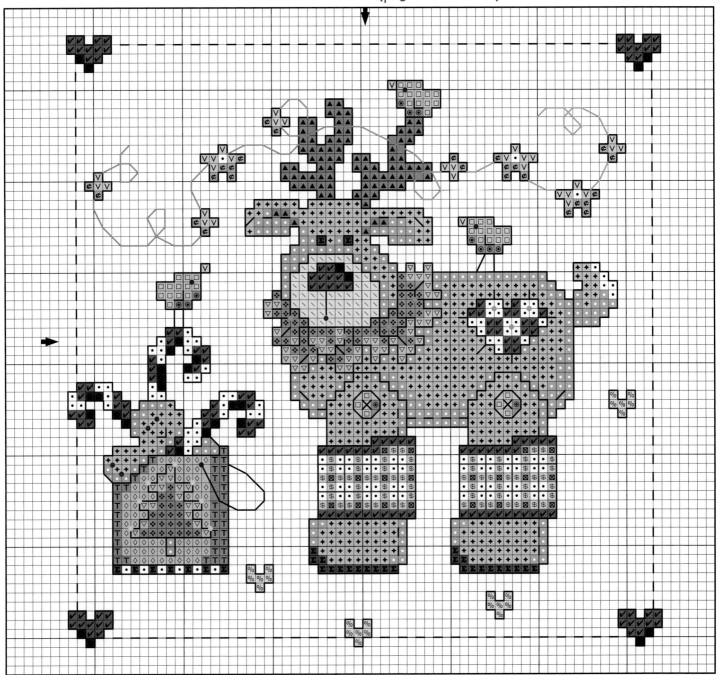

Reindeer (67w x 67h)

X	DMC	1/4X	B'ST	ANC.
•	blanc			2
■	304		⊘	1006
✔	321			9046
T	341			117
▲	434			310
◉	435	◪		1046
✦	436	◪		1045
%	605			1094
◥	739			387
▣	813	◪		161
◉	826	◪		161
✤	910			229

X	DMC	B'ST	ANC.
▽	912		209
$	959		186
◼	3371	⊘	382
◇	3747		120
⊠	3812	⊘	188
¢	3820		306
V	3822		295
◉	304 Fr. Knot		
●	3371 Fr. Knot		
◉	3812 Fr. Knot		
○	3822 Fr. Knot		

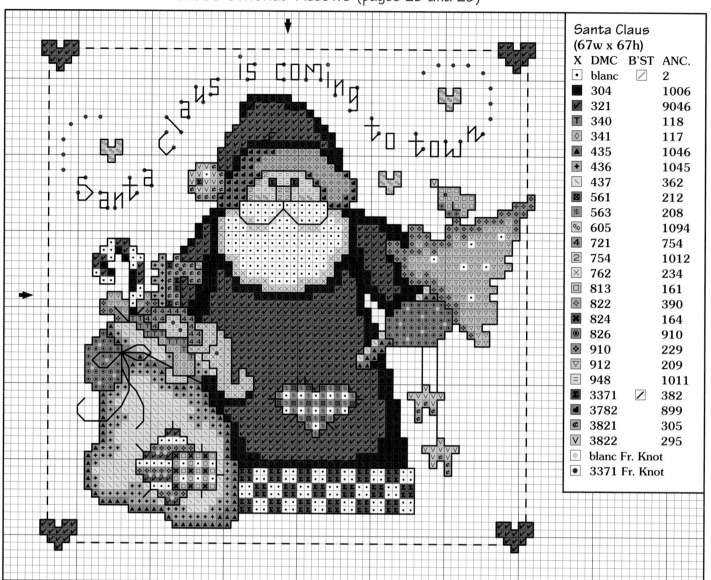

Santa Claus
(67w x 67h)

X	DMC	B'ST	ANC.
·	blanc	⟋	2
■	304		1006
✓	321		9046
T	340		118
◇	341		117
▲	435		1046
✦	436		1045
◺	437		362
⊠	561		212
$	563		208
%	605		1094
4	721		754
2	754		1012
✕	762		234
☐	813		161
◈	822		390
✖	824		164
◉	826		910
✤	910		229
▽	912		209
=	948		1011
Σ	3371	⟋	382
◢	3782		899
¢	3821		305
V	3822		295
○	blanc Fr. Knot		
●	3371 Fr. Knot		

REINDEER SWEATSHIRT
(page 63)

139

BUTTON LAMP
(page 50)

SNOWMAN TABLE RUNNER,
STAR PLACE CARD
STAR NAPKIN RING & NAPKIN
TINY STOCKINGS & STAR TREE
(pages 32 and 33)

FESTIVE POTS
(pages 34 and 35)

SNOWMAN BOX
(page 70)

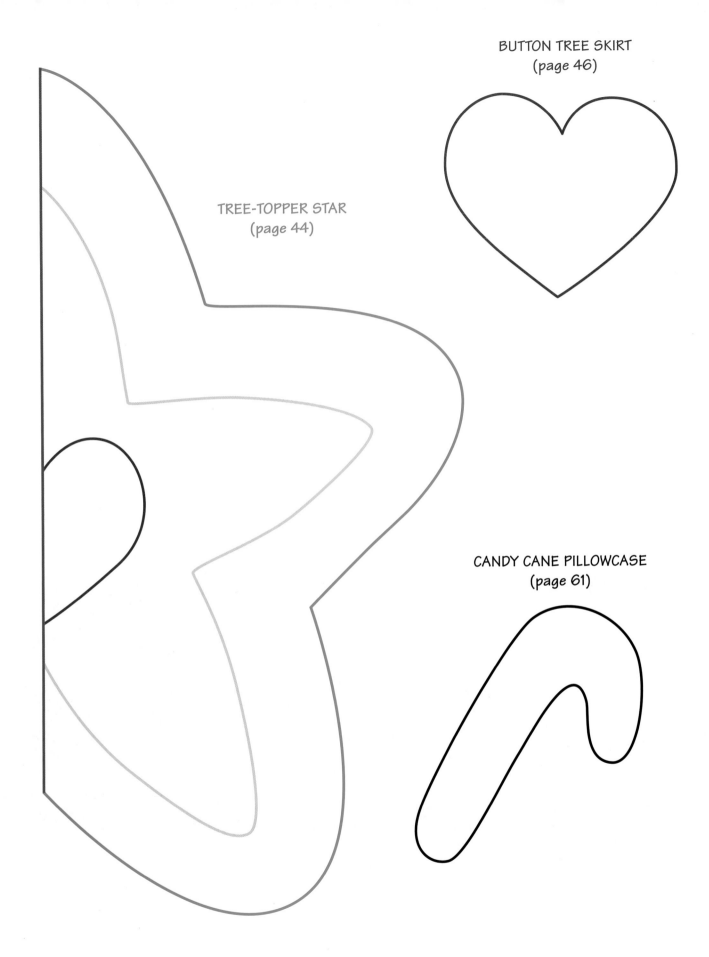

BUTTON TREE SKIRT
(page 46)

TREE-TOPPER STAR
(page 44)

CANDY CANE PILLOWCASE
(page 61)

PAPER EDGINGS
(pages 42 and 43)

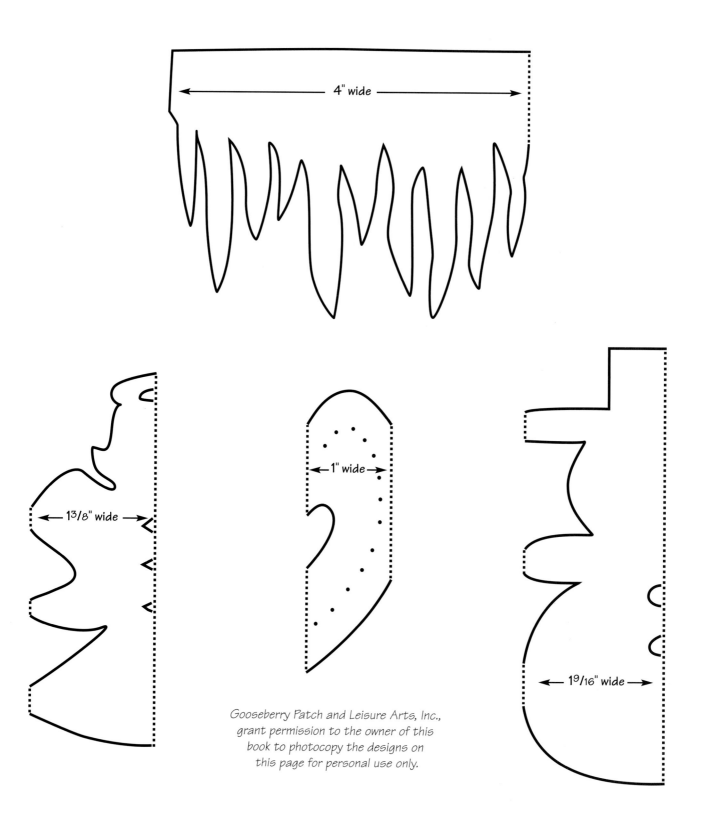

4" wide

1⅜" wide

1" wide

1⁹/₁₆" wide

Gooseberry Patch and Leisure Arts, Inc., grant permission to the owner of this book to photocopy the designs on this page for personal use only.

143

star A
(cut 1)

beard
(cut 1)

star B
(cut 1)

tree trunk A
(cut 1)

mitten
(cut 2)

face
(cut 1)

tree A
(cut 1)

tree trunk 2
(cut 1)

coat & hat
(cut 1)

tree B
(cut 2)

boots
(cut 1)

144

wings A
(cut 2)

star A
(cut 1)

star B
(cut 1)

wings B
(cut 1)

robe B
(cut 2)

robe A
(cut 1)

star C
(cut 2)

head
(cut 3)

sleeve
(cut 3)

feet
(cut 3 each)

hand
(cut 3)

tree A
(cut 1)

tree trunk
(cut 2)

tree B
(cut 1)

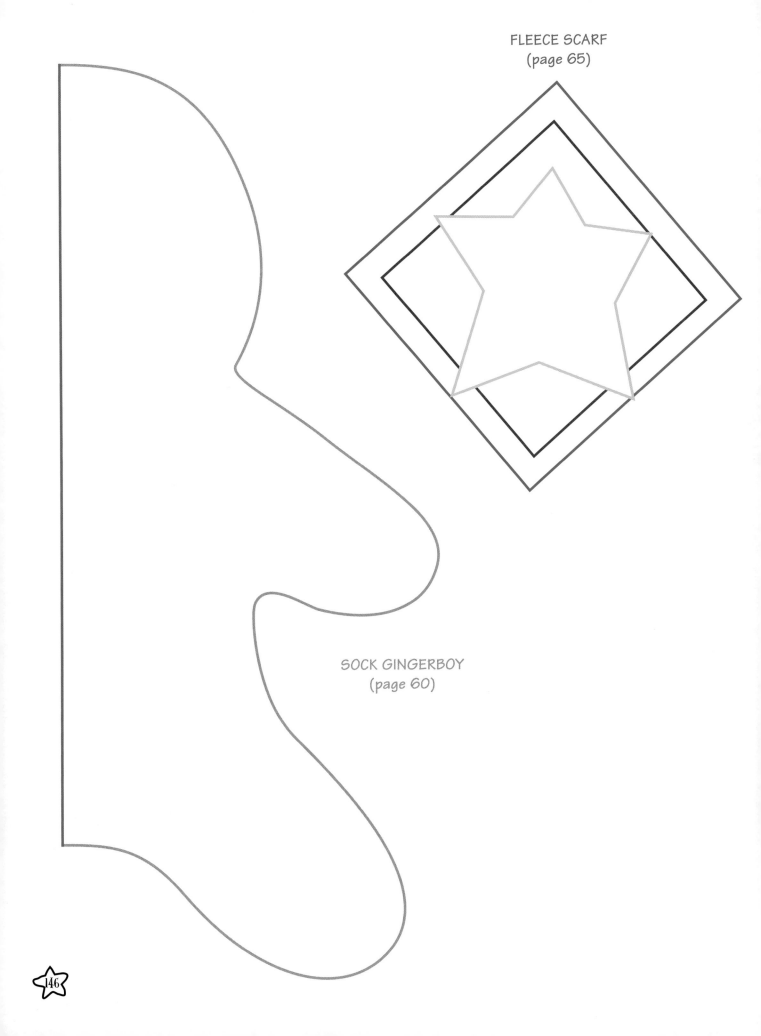

FLEECE SCARF
(page 65)

SOCK GINGERBOY
(page 60)

146

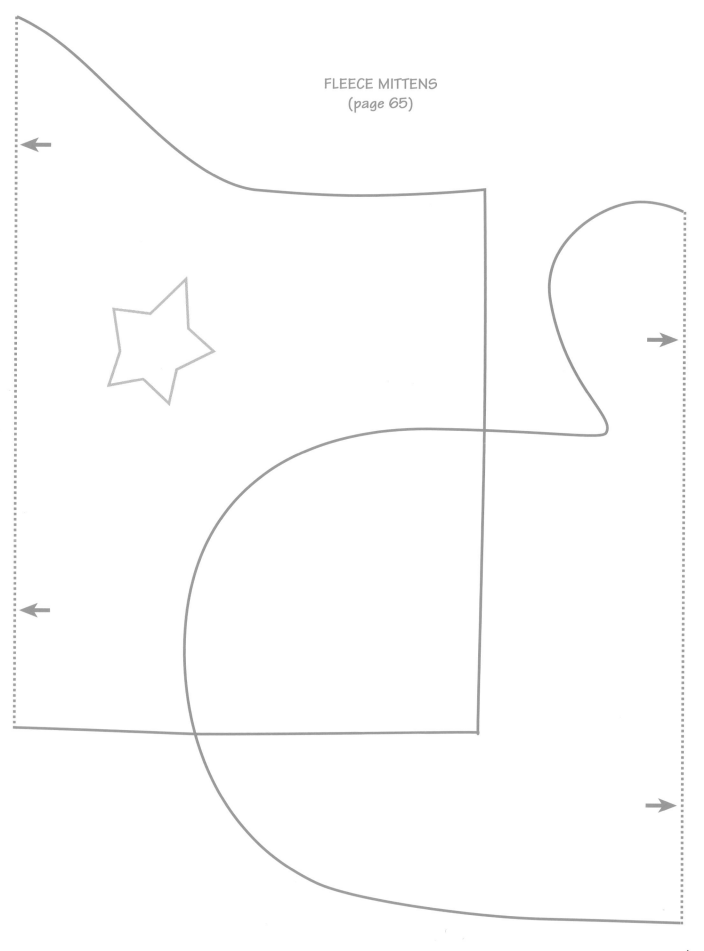

FLEECE MITTENS
(page 65)

MOOSE THROW
(page 67)

148

SNOWMAN THROW
(page 66)

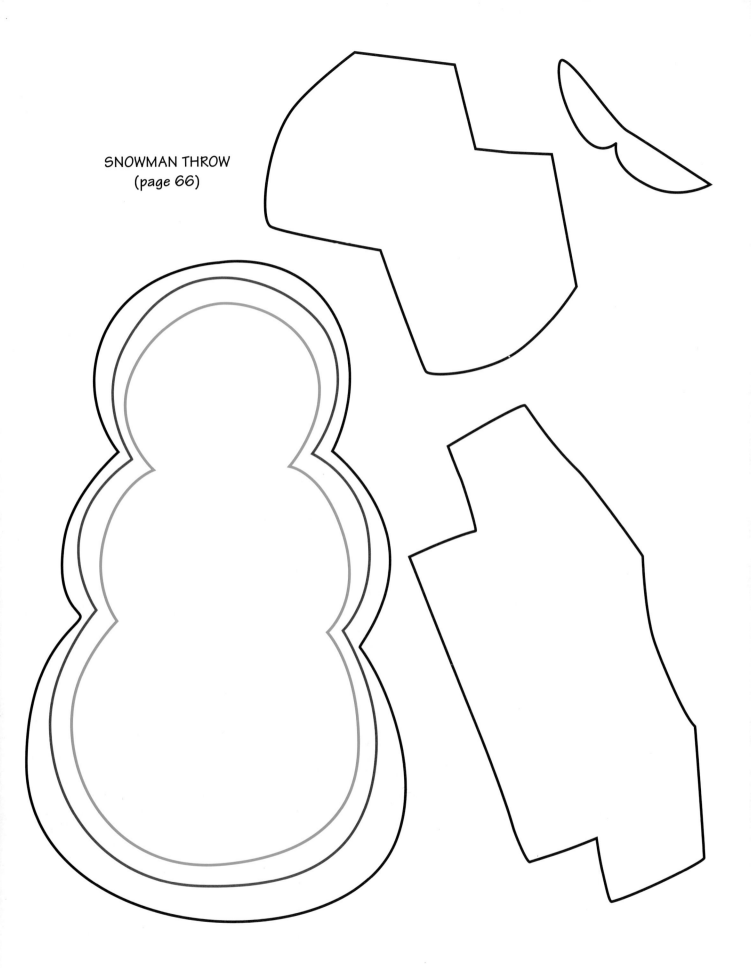

GINGERBREAD MAN & HEART THROW
(page 67)

MITTEN COASTERS
(page 82)

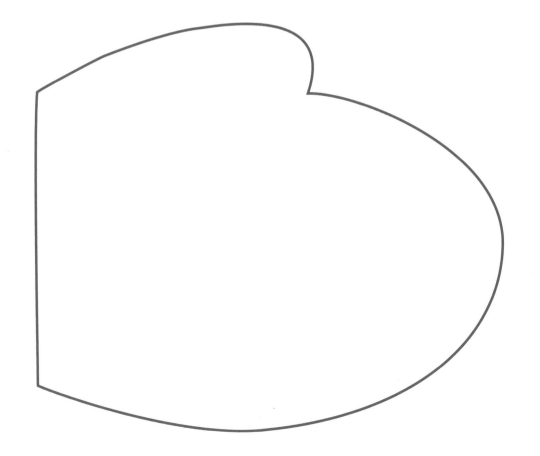

Friendship
is
the thread
that ties

together.

Friendship Frame
(page 70)

and precious are all things that come from
FRIENDS.

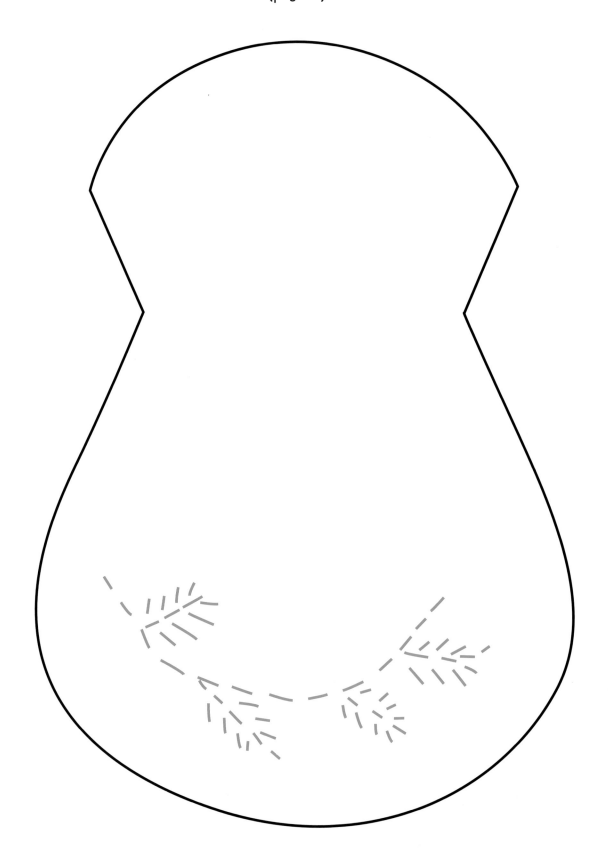

STOCKING TAG
(page 85)

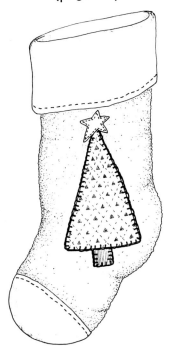

GARDEN HERB BREAD BLEND
(page 83)

CHILL-CHASER CHILI
(page 77)

Chill-Chaser Chili

1 pkg. bean mix
1 lb. lean ground beef
¼ c. onion, chopped
¼ c. green pepper, chopped
28 oz. can stewed tomatoes
Seasoning packet
1 to 2 c. water

Soak beans overnight in 5 c. water or cover with cold water in a saucepan and boil for 10 minutes. Cover pan and turn off heat. Let beans sit 1 hour, then drain. Cover with fresh water and simmer beans for 60 to 90 minutes 'til tender. Drain and set aside. Brown beef with onion and green pepper 'til meat is no longer pink. Drain. Add tomatoes, seasoning packet and water. Simmer for 1 to 1½ hours. Add beans - simmer additional 30 to 60 minutes.
... ★ serves 6 ★ ...

"YOU'RE AN ANGEL" BAG
(page 75)

TAGS & LABELS
(page 81)

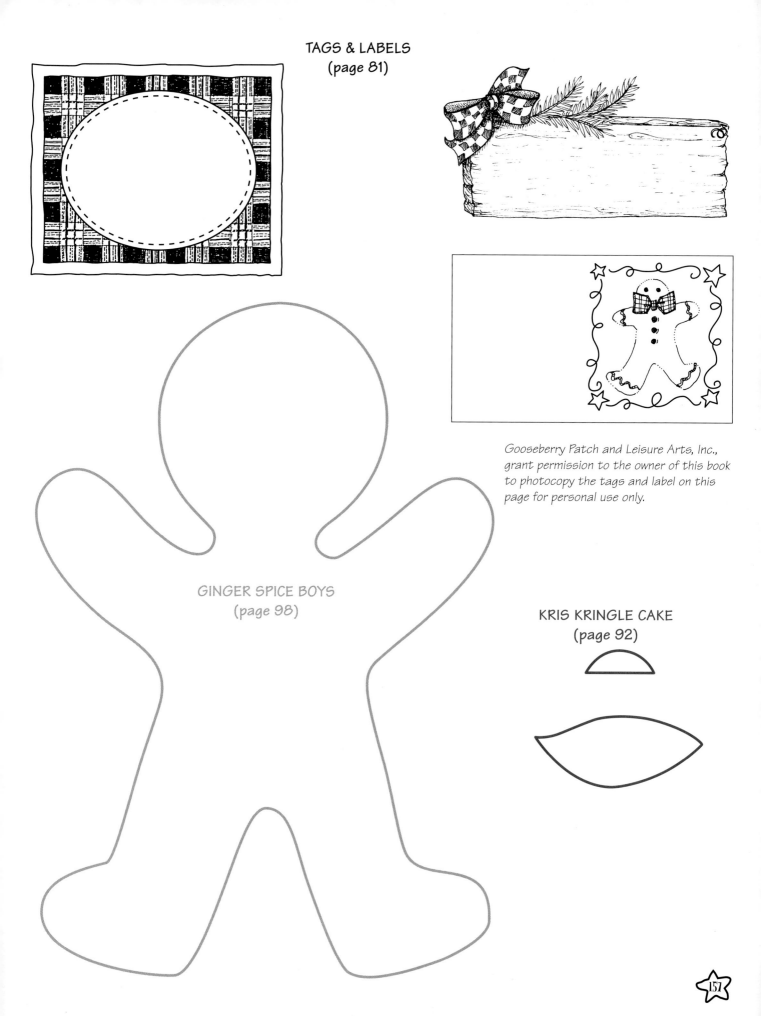

GINGER SPICE BOYS
(page 98)

KRIS KRINGLE CAKE
(page 92)

PROJECT INDEX

RECIPE INDEX